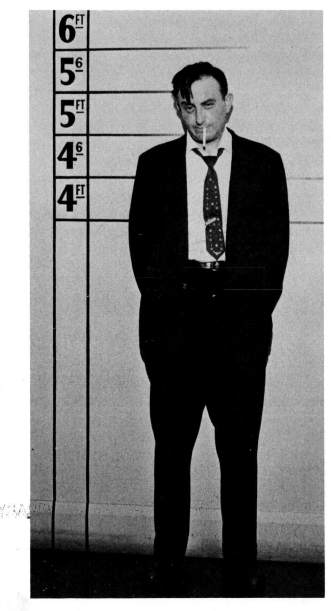

Figure 1. Photograph of author taken at conclusion of an undercover case. It was necessary to arrest the author to prevent his identity from becoming known.

UNDERCOVER

By

CARMINE J. MOTTO

Special Agent in Charge, Retired
New York Special Detail
United States Secret Service

CHARLES C THOMAS • PUBLISHER

Springfield • Illinois • U.S.A

Published and Distributed Throughout the World by

CHARLES C THOMAS • PUBLISHER

Bannerstone House

301-327 East Lawrence Avenue, Springfield, Illinois, U.S.A.

Natchez Plantation House

735 North Atlantic Boulevard, Fort Lauderdale, Florida, U.S.A.

*With THOMAS BOOKS careful attention is given to all details of
manufacturing and design. It is the Publisher's desire to present books that are
satisfactory as to their physical qualities and artistic possibilities and
appropriate for their particular use. THOMAS BOOKS will be true to those
laws of quality that assure a good name and good will.*

Printed in the United States of America
RN-1

To Flora and Irene

PREFACE

Undercover work and handling informants, at
best, are hit and miss affairs. They will never become exact
sciences unless someone works wonders with a computer. The
experienced officer who has handled many informants and the
officer who has done much undercover work are soon recognized as experts in their field and it is men of this caliber that
are expected to break in new officers who are anxious to
become efficient in all phases of police work.

In reading this book, it will be noted very early that most all
the experiences related are successful ones. It is not to be
construed that all undercover cases end in success, on the con-
trary, most cases are failures. A 30 or 35 per cent average would
be considered excellent. Most times, we know why we are
successful; but it is very difficult to learn why we fail. The
failures would fill volumes while the successes might barely fill a
book.

Sometimes it is obvious why we fail, an informant double-
crosses us, an agent is recognized, a tail is made. For various
reasons, the suspect cannot produce and sometimes he has no
intention of producing, he is merely trying to pull a swindle.
There are times when there is no apparent reason for the failure
and we can only guess what went wrong. We cannot learn from
our mistakes unless we know we made mistakes and can recognize them and then take the necessary steps to prevent them
from happening again. There are times when we have to wait
weeks and sometimes months before the informant can learn
through his own sources what went wrong in the case.

In this book, I prefer calling all people who give information
"informants." The words "stool," "rat," "squealer," and "informer" are all words that belong to another era and have no
place in modern-day police work. Informants are one of the

principal tools of the police, and like all journeymen who must use tools, the police too must realize their importance when a job has to be done.

Informants must be cultivated, cajoled, rewarded, respected and reinterviewed often. We recognize our informants for what they are and treat them accordingly.

The stories related in this book are not told for the sake of spinning yarns. I sincerely hope that they will give the reader a better understanding of the principles that are outlined. These experiences could have been handled differently by other undercover agents, and perhaps still have been successful.

I do not expect that everyone will agree with all that I have attempted to outline, that is understandable. This book was written without any research whatsoever. It is the recounting of experiences over a long period of time.

Most of the cases discussed in this book are Secret Service cases, and I think it would be presumptuous of me to cite cases of other agencies or departments. However, I feel that the principles are the same and by changing the type of contraband, you will include all types of undercover work performed by various agencies.

Most of my experiences in undercover work involved counterfeiting of currency, checks, bonds and other types of government obligations. However, in doing undercover work, an agent sometimes has to make purchases of contraband that belong under the jurisdiction of another agency.

The cooperation of all agencies over the years has been splendid and it is this type of cooperation that is needed to wage a successful fight against organized crime.

The words, "undercover agent" as used in this text, are meant to be all-inclusive. They refer to the undercover federal agent, state trooper, deputy sheriff, detective and any law enforcement officer who is working undercover. Years ago, when I was a young agent, undercover work was known as "roping" and the man doing the work was the "roper." The term is rarely used today and the undercover agent has replaced the roper in words only. Some of the finest undercover work was accomplished by old-time ropers who gave their lives in the interest of law enforcement activities.

In narrating cases, I have purposely omitted using times, dates, places and names. I have no desire to identify any informant who has worked for me in the past, neither do I desire to identify any man who has violated the law, has paid his debt to society and perhaps is now leading a clean and useful life. In rare instances where a name is used, it is because the person has died or has publicly told the story himself and does not wish to remain anonymous.

Those who have grown in the hierarchy of the underworld are being given the necessary attention by the various agencies and any arrest should be for a crime that is being committed and not for something that was done years and years ago.

I have attempted to do everything possible not to make this a handbook on how to "beat the law." I have always felt that experiences of the "old-timers" are something that is sorely needed by the young up-coming officers of today who can profit by the cases that have been successful in the past and these cases should not be laid to rest with the men who made them. Some of the famous police textbooks of the past have been in print for thirty to thirty-five years and are as useful today to the new officers as when they were written.

I have purposely omitted the names of other agents who worked with me on various cases. Again, this would necessitate a lot of research into old files. Some of these agents will someday perhaps write their own books. Their experiences are strictly their own, especially the undercover cases they worked on. For another person to write of their experiences would be a second-hand account of something that should be told first-hand.

Attempting to dedicate a book after thirty-five years of police work becomes extremely difficult. The man who gave you your first chance; the informant who helped give you a reputation; the teachers in the various schools; the men you worked with; the men who worked under you; your family who had to put up with your continual and extended absences; the district attorneys who successfully prosecuted your cases; all your brother officers, city, state and federal, who cooperated with you even though they knew the case was not theirs; the unsung witnesses who gave testimony in spite of the fact they might later be in some danger — all these people, and perhaps many more, should be given the credit, because without them, there is no truly successful police officer and no successful fight against crime.

I would like to single out Director James J. Rowley of the United States Secret Service whom I am proud to call a contemporary. He had the foresight over the years to see the need for training more and more men in the art of undercover work and thereby kept a strangle hold on the modern-day counterfeiter.

CARMINE J. MOTTO

INTRODUCTION

UNDERCOVER work or roping is probably the most fascinating of all police work. It is a challange to the roping agent to use his capabilities to the utmost in order to match wits with the underworld. Undercover work is best described as a *drama* involving three participants: a) the informant, b) the suspect and c) the roping agent.

The purpose of undercover work is to gain knowledge of the criminal and to gather evidence against him; and to locate the source of the crime and obtain enough evidence against the suspect for a conviction. The goal of the undercover agent will vary depending on the department he is working for. In a counterfeit case, he is striving to locate the plant (the printer); in an alcohol case he is trying to locate the still; in a narcotics case he is attempting to locate the person or persons responsible for bringing the drugs into this country or locality. In the cases mentioned above, the goal is usually accomplished by the roping agent making a "buy" direct from the suspect with the intention of convincing the suspect to cooperate with the agency, after he has been caught in the act of committing a crime and learns he has been dealing with a government agent or police official. Modern undercover work, as employed by the various agencies today, in addition to the introduction of more sophisticated electronic devices, will undoubtedly be the ultimate weapons to combat organized crime.

CONTENTS

UNDERCOVER

Chapter 1

THE INFORMANT

THE informant is usually the start of an under-cover case. He is precisely described as "one who gives information." He is a very necessary part of police work and most agencies would be at a loss to operate without him.

MOTIVATION

It must always be kept in mind that the informant has a motive for informing and it is imperative for the roping agent to know what the informant's motive is. Without knowing his motive, it would be nearly impossible to work with him, as his expectations may be far greater than the agency could afford. It would be beneficial to look into some of the reasons *why* a person informs.

Profit

Some people inform for profit. The informant in this case has information to sell and he naturally will try to get the most amount of money for his information. This usually creates a problem, one which has to be worked out with the informant, either by the supervisor or the roping agent, before the case is worked on. Some professional informants will have a preconceived idea of how much money their information is worth, either by asking for a percentage of the recovery or by placing a flat amount for their services. The amount that the informant expects is, in most cases, far more than the agency will want to pay.

Very often in counterfeiting cases, the informants ask for 10 per cent of the recovery. While 10 per cent does not sound like much, in a case of a million dollar seizure of counterfeit notes, this will give the informant 100,000 dollars, which is an amount that has nver been paid to any informant. Even 1 per cent would be 10,000 dollars in a million dollar seizure — this is also a lot of money.

In cases of counterfeit seizures, a percentage generally cannot be worked out because the informant does not know how much money there is in the plant and a percentage would be far more than the government can allow.

In cases involving smuggling or in cases where the government recovers something of value, 10 per cent would probably be a fair amount. Here, it must be kept in mind that the government actually receives something of value, but in a case involving counterfeit money, the government gets nothing but worthless paper.

In counterfeiting cases, an amount is agreed upon for the services of the informant and generally this amount will increase if a larger seizure is made than anticipated. If a counterfeiting plant is seized with a large amount of counterfeit money, a considerable amount can be paid to the informant. A supervisor, in trying to arrive at a fair amount to pay an informant, must take the following into consideration: How long has the plant been operating? Who are the people behind the plant? What is the amount of the seizure? How good is the counterfeit note? How much of it has been passed successfully? How many investigators is this note tying up on the street? How much money is available for rewards before the end of the fiscal year? In considering the above questions, a supervisor or agent can safely arrive at a figure to pay the informant. The money is generally paid to him immediately after the case is made. It is not practical in this type of case to wait until the case has been successfully prosecuted. This could sometimes take several years.

Some agencies find that it is profitable to keep informants on the payroll, giving them money on a weekly or monthly basis. The informant in turn supplies the agency with information. This arrangement works out very well where the department involved is interested in all types of crimes, such as local police or the Federal Bureau of Investigation. However, for organizations like the Secret

Service, Alcohol, Tobacco and Firearms Division and United States Customs, the work is specialized and very often an informant is a "one shotter." He runs into this information and reports it. Some informants have given the Secret Service counterfeiting information and have never again run into another counterfeiting case, not because they were not looking for it but because the crime is not that prevalent.

Revenge

Some informants inform because they want revenge. For reasons best known to themselves, they want to see the violators arrested either because it suits their particular purpose to have the violator put in jail or because of something that the violator did to the informant for which he wants revenge. The spirit of revenge that motivates this type of informant is very strong and generally the informant will extend himself to the utmost to see that the case is made.

In the middle 1950's the Secret Service was plagued with counterfeit government checks in and around the southwest portion of the country. One of the agents received information from an informant that a local prostitute was handling the counterfeit government checks for a group of violators that controlled prostitutes in that particular area.

I was assigned to work on this case and I proceeded to a small town in the southwest and met the informant. The informant agreed to introduce me to the girl that was handling the counterfeit checks and agreed to help me make a purchase from her.

I spent two or three hours with the informant and could not make up my mind why he was informing. Several more meetings with the informant were necessary before I finally found out what motivated him. It was learned that he was a pimp and at one time controlled prostitution in that area. The people handling the counterfeit checks had "strong-armed" all the girls and they were successful in taking control away from the informant. The informant knew if he could have the opposition arrested on the counterfeiting charges, he would again be able to control prostitution in the whole county.

The introduction was made a short time later and I was able to buy fifty checks from the prostitute, I then put in an order for one thousand checks and she explained that it would take two or three weeks before a delivery could be made. She could not explain why it would take that long except to say that the checks came from very far away.

I made several meetings with the girl and on each occasion she asked me a lot of questions about myself and I told her I was "on the lam" from New York and could not return until I was advised by my people that it would be safe to return. The purchase of one thousand checks involved a considerable amount of money and some of the moves that she was making could not be explained.

Several days after my meeting with her, the sheriff of the particular county where we were operating received information from a confidential source that a gangster from New York was in town with a lot of money and that a group of people were going to sell him some counterfeit checks but instead of turning the government checks over to him, they were going to murder him and take his money. The sheriff did not know how good his information was but it tied in perfectly with the case I was working on and it was decided that this would be a good time for me to leave the area because of the stalling tactics of the group.

I had a final meeting with the girl and I made sure she had an undercover telephone number where I could be reached. Then I told her I was going back to New York because I did not believe her group could produce one thousand checks. She tried very hard to get me to stay. I insisted that I could not stay any longer, that my people wanted me to return.

Several days later, I received a telephone call from a man who identified himself as a friend of the prostitute. He stated that the checks were ready and suggested that I come down immediately to get them. I told him that my people were no longer interested and did not trust his group. He explained that they had a lot of trouble producing the checks but that they were now ready and the whole deal could be consummated within twenty-four hours. I again told him that our deal was dead.

Then I told him that I knew a Chinese merchant who was on his way to the Philippines, that this merchant was very wealthy and that he would undoubtedly be interested in purchasing the checks. I stated, however, that this man would not budge from his own home to make the deal as he would be afraid of a stick up, further that he did not fly and was going cross-country by railroad. He then suggested that we meet halfway like Cleveland or Chicago. I suggested New York and after several telephone calls, Washington, D. C. was agreed upon as the place of delivery.

We all met at the airport in Washington, D. C., where the suspects were arrested after turning over the checks to me. They were armed and also had samples of bank checks, driver's licenses, and Social Security cards to show me for future sales.

After the arrest, one of the men broke down and stated that the counterfeits were made in Durango, Mexico. A detail was sent to Mexico to work with the police. In a short time, the printer was identified, the plant was seized and all who were involved in the operation were arrested.

This is a classic example of an informant giving good information because it suited his purpose to have the opposition taken out of circulation.

Concealment of a Crime

Many people become informants after they have committed a crime and fear that the police are in the process of having them identified. They feel that if they inform, the police will either forget the violation or have it reduced because of the information that they give. This type of informant is hard to identify because he generally will not admit that he committed the crime or that he is trying to conceal it. One of the better cases broken by the Secret Service was accomplished because of an informant who fitted in this category.

One day a man whom we will call Pete came into the New York Office of the Secret Service with a package containing 75,000 dollars in counterfeit twenty dollar bills. These counterfeits originated in Chicago, Illinois, and were being circulated throughout the whole country in very large amounts. The informant told the agent in charge that he was given this package to take overseas;

that he was to exchange the counterfeit money for narcotics and return to the United States with the narcotics which he was to turn over to the man who gave him the counterfeits.

The informant has a responsible job aboard a United States merchant vessel. He told the agent in charge that he could not go through with the deal and wanted to bow out. He stated he would surrender the counterfeits but would not give any further information.

At about this time, I received a telephone call in the office from a girl who stated she had been victimized on a counterfeit twenty dollars by a man who had spent the night with her. This girl came down to the office, stated she was a prostitute and that she had been paid the previous night with two counterfeit twenty dollar bills. She gave a description of the man who stayed with her and stated that he was a seaman and would recognize him if she saw him again.

Her description of the passer was identical with Pete who was still in the office insisting that he would not help the Service any further. The girl was allowed to view Pete and we had all we could do to hold her after she identified him as the passer. This, of course, put the informant into an entirely different category. He was no longer a willing informant but instead a potential defendant.

After the informant was told that he was going to be placed under arrest, he decided to fully cooperate with us. He stated that a man by the name of Lewis whom he had known in Chicago was now controlling the lottery racket in Savannah, Georgia; that Lewis was able to obtain these counterfeit notes from a contact in Chicago; that Lewis wanted the informant to take the notes overseas and bring back narcotics which Lewis could distribute among his own connections.

Lewis had a very bad reputation and was considered a violent man. The informant feared him and would not testify against him nor would he introduce an undercover agent to him. We prevailed upon the informant to make a telephone call to Lewis and to advise Lewis that there was a little heat in the New York port; that Pete was afraid to take the money overseas; that he was going to return the counterfeit money to Lewis by a trusted messenger.

Pete did contact Lewis and the conversation was monitored.

Lewis warned Pete that he would be killed if he tried to return the money to Savannah. He repeated it three times to make sure Pete understood. He told the informant that if he did not want to carry the notes overseas, he should send them to a man named Kulik in Chicago.

A quick check on Kulik revealed that he was a cab driver in Chicago; that he did not have a criminal record and apparently worked for a living and was a good family man.

Sending the notes to Kulik would not make a case. The agent in charge, after a conversation with the informant, told me to take the notes to Savannah; return them to Lewis and then place Lewis under arrest after he accepted the notes.

I proceeded to Savannah, Georgia, and went to a local bar where Lewis was known to hang out. Before going to the bar, I had deposited the counterfeit notes in a safe deposit box at a local hotel.

After several hours of waiting, Lewis showed up at the bar and when he heard that a man from New York wanted to see him, he immediately went into a rage surmising that this had something to do with the counterfeit money. Upon meeting me, he demanded to know who I was and who sent me. I told him I was from New York; that Pete had taken a rap for me on the west coast several years ago and that I owed Pete a favor. Pete asked me to bring a package to Lewis; that it was very important and that I should pick up all my expense money from Lewis.

There was much conversation between Lewis and me about the package. It was apparent that he did not want to take the package. I finally told him I would take the package and keep it myself. The package represented at least a ten thousand dollar investment for Lewis and he was not anxious to lose this money. He finally agreed to take the package and pay me for my expenses.

He accompanied me to the hotel, where I picked up the package and handed it to him. He accepted it and was immediately placed under arrest. Lewis, true to his reputation, did not cooperate and remained mute all through the questioning. His defense was to be that he accepted the package from me thinking it was a gift from a seaman friend.

While we were in town, we decided to question a friend of Lewis' named Fred who we had reason to believe was involved. Fred ran an aviation school and we knew he flew Lewis to Chicago on many occasions. Fred proved to be very cooperative. He took us to a place in the woods where he had hidden over 100,000 dollars worth of counterfeit notes. After he heard that Lewis was arrested, he got rid of these notes because he felt that he would be questioned and his premises searched. He admitted flying Lewis to Chicago when Lewis picked up the counterfeit money. He also went with Lewis to the man's house who supplied the counterfeit money to Lewis. From the description given by Fred, the unknown man could be none other than "Satan."

Satan had been the scourge of the Service for many years and everyone was anxious to make a case against him.

We flew to Chicago with Fred in one of his planes and while there, we gave Fred an opportunity to surreptitiously view Satan. Fred identified Satan as the source of the notes. We decided to wait until the grand jury convened in Savannah and attempt to indict Satan and then arrest him.

On the morning that the grand jury met, I was asked by the United States Attorney to see what was keeping Fred as he was our lead-off witness. I walked down the street to where Fred operated a shop and arrived about one minute after Fred shot himself in the head. He died immediately and the case against Satan "went out the window." He was not apprehended until several years later and he too met a violent end.

Eventually, Lewis went to trial and his lawyers fought hard to get the jury to believe that Lewis was the victim of government entrapment. The lawyers pulled no punches and attempted to smear me by making reference to my ethnic background and suggest to the jury that perhaps I had received the counterfeits from some of my relatives in New York. The trial was bitter from start to finish, finally it went to the jury. They were out about seven minutes and returned with a verdict of guilty. Lewis was immediately sentenced to serve fifteen years. He came out of jail some years later, a broken man, his family had left him, he had an incurable disease and died very shortly after being released.

This case would have probably never been made if the

informant had not become hungry and passed several counterfeit notes before shipping out. He had committed a crime and when he felt that the prostitute might have recognized him and knew enough about him to identify him, he decided to become an informant, hoping that he would not be arrested for the passing of the notes.

Assistance in Another Criminal Matter

A great percentage of informants are motivated to inform in order to help themselves in another criminal matter. They feel that by informing they can make a deal with the agency to help them either in another court case or to have their cooperation brought before a sentencing judge on another matter.

One of the largest counterfeiting cases ever made in New York was made because a man needed help in a criminal matter, not for himself but for his brother who was arrested with him.

The two Esposito brothers were arrested when they were caught in the act of selling counterfeit money to an undercover agent. The buy itself was only several thousand dollars, but the interesting fact was that one brother immediately wanted to make a deal, as long as something could be done for the other brother. The older brother, Al, explained that Frank, the younger brother, was a narcotic addict and that he had a narcotic matter pending in another court. He asked that his brother be released and if this were done, he would take the agents to a spot where there was more counterfeit money than any of us had ever seen in our lives. I explained to him that something could be done the following day but that night his brother had to go to jail.

Al pleaded that Frank would need a "fix" during the night and by morning he would be going through the withdrawals. I told Al that the Detention Headquarters would undoubtedly give Frank something to help him through the night.

The following morning, both brothers were ready for arraignment. As predicted, Frank did not look too well and this gave Al much concern. Al was ready to do most anything to help his brother. We received permission to postpone the arraignment until we could check out the information that Al wanted to give.

His first story was that he had purchased the counterfeit notes at two dollars per hundred from an unknown person. I knew that Al had been selling the notes for as cheap as five dollars per hundred and it just did not make sense. I insisted that he level with me, also that all deals were off until he told the truth. It took some convincing but before long, Al was ready to tell us how he got the notes.

He told of a distant relative who was holding a large sum of counterfeits for a group who were desperate to find a hiding place for their notes as they were experiencing a lot of "heat" as the results of friends who were arrested. They prevailed on Al's relative to keep the money in a storage bin in his cellar. He lived in a four-family house, he was a working man, he did not have a criminal record, so the mob thought he would be a safe person to leave the money with. Al's relative, whom we shall call Pepe, kept the money as requested but he made one mistake and that was taking Al into his confidence.

Al was a fairly good burglar. When Pepe and his wife went to work, Al went into the cellar and examined all the storage bins till he found the one with the cartons and suitcases full of counterfeit money. Being small, Al was able to squeeze through an opening on top of the bin and help himself to a portion of the money. Al did not know anything about counterfeit money and was happy to sell it at five dollars a hundred. The customers were plentiful and so were his trips to the cellar. Al made out fairly well until he had the misfortune of selling a load of the counterfeits to an undercover agent. This led to his present predicament.

It was obvious that neither Al nor his brother could afford to cooperate any further. The only other thing that Al could do was to identify the spot where the money was and name his relative. He did this within minutes of his cooperation.

It was necessary for us to move as quickly as possible. We knew as soon as the news of Al and Frank's arrest became known, the money would undoubtedly be moved. We applied for a search warrant on the basis of confidential information we had obtained. The warrant was issued by a United States Commissioner for the search of the storage bin in Pepe's apartment house.

The warrant was served shortly after Pepe arrived home from

work. I told Pepe that I had a warrant for the search of his cellar. He asked what I was searching for and I said counterfeit money. He said, "I guess you know all about, follow me." He let myself and two other agents down the cellar. He opened the storage bin and led us to over one million dollars that was packed in cartons and suitcases. Pepe was immediately placed under arrest. He was questioned and he stated that he had stolen the notes from the basement of a home he was working in.

He stated he was a plumber and when he worked in this particular cellar, he saw some cartons. Being alone he looked in the cartons and found it contained a large amount of what looked like money. He determined it was counterfeit and when the people were out, he let himself into the cellar and stole the cartons of notes.

He claimed he could no longer remember where the home was. He recalled it was somewhere in New Jersey and he was sure he could never find the place again. I asked him when this occurred and he answered sometime in July or August. He insisted that he placed the notes in his cellar and never went near them again. I told him he was lying. He insisted he was not. I asked him to explain how the notes became wrapped in newspaper which was dated six months after he put them in the cellar. He asked for a few minutes and stated he would think of an answer. Sure enough he did. He stated on one occasion he went to the cellar, took some notes out, wrapped them in newspaper and then in a gift box. He put the box under the Christmas tree as his wife's present. He claimed that he did this just for a lark. Well, we asked the question and received an answer.

It looked like we had a perfect case against Pepe. He hired an expensive lawyer who immediately made a motion to suppress the evidence as the search warrant was not legal. A hearing was held before a federal judge. He listened to the facts in the case and ruled that there was not enough probable cause to obtain the warrant. He castigated the agents and the United States Attorney for moving too rapidly and not taking enough time to prepare the case. The fact that the press was about to print the information that the arrest of the brothers was made, the fact that the money could be moved momentarily did not phase the good judge. His prerogative to throw out the search is not being argued but to castigate the investigators was almost too much to swallow. After it was over, we were thankful that the judge did not go one step further and make us return the money to Pepe. Even though we received a bad break, there was no doubt that taking over a million dollars out of circulation was a great help to the merchants around the area who could have been victimized with these counterfeits.

The Service eventually brought Al's cooperation to the attention of the judge handling both matters and he and his brother were given a short prison term. His brother eventually was sent to a Federal institution where he was able to kick the narcotic habit.

This is merely one example of how violators will cooperate fully with authorities when they feel they will be helped in another criminal matter. In these cases, it is very important to find out in advance how serious their problems are. Some informants have a habit of only telling part of the story and when the time comes to help them, it is learned that their violations were far more serious than originally believed. In one case, a man stated that he needed help because he assaulted a man. It developed that the man died and the charge against the informant was manslaughter for which he was to serve twenty years. He was on appeal bond when he came to us. It was originally thought that an assault would be relatively simple matter to assist him in. Needless to say, nothing was done for him and he was not used.

Good Citizenship

There comes a time in an investigator's life when a good citizen approaches him with important criminal information. Unless the investigator is experienced, he might not handle this person properly. The informant comes to him in an awkward manner. He generally does not speak in the vernacular of the underworld and at times appears naive. This type of an informant is a gem and must be handled carefully. All efforts must be made to see that he is not exposed and everything possible must be done to make him feel that he is the good citizen that he is.

A good citizen was responsible for breaking one of the largest counterfeiting cases in the South. He had no angle other than to

Figure 2. Million-dollar seizure of counterfeit notes from cellar. At right, Special Agent in Charge, Al Wong.

report what he had seen and heard to the proper authorities. Let's call this man Jim Thompson. He ran a small jewelry store in a city in the deep South. One night, just before closing time, a man entered the store and engaged Jim in a conversation. After a short time, the man whom we shall call Al Davis showed Jim a twenty dollar bill and asked Jim what he thought of it. Jim said it looked all right to him. Al said it was counterfeit and that they were just printed and he could get all he wanted. He asked Jim if he could get in touch with some people up North that he knew and maybe a sale could be made. Al left a sample with Jim and said he would be back the following Monday to find out if they could do business.

Jim immediately reported the matter to the local FBI who in turn notified our local office. An examination of the sample proved it to be a new counterfeit that had not as yet been put in circulation.

I was given the assignment of going down to meet Jim Thompson with a view to making a purchase of the counterfeit notes from Al Davis. I arrived in the city fairly early on Monday morning and after arranging several rooms at a hotel and obtaining the necessary coverage from the local police and our people, I immediately went to the jewelry store and introduced myself to Jim. Jim just started to explain what happened the previous Friday and in the middle of the conversation, Al Davis walked in. I hurriedly asked Jim to introduce me to Al and say that I was his friend from up North. Jim played his part to perfection and after the introduction, he left the two of us in the back of the store and went about his business

Davis took several of the counterfeits from his pocket and showed them to me. He stated he could get them in any amounts and he wanted a price of fifteen dollars per hundred. I told Davis that I only had 1500 dollars in cash with me, that I would pick up a package to take back up North and would return in a day or so to make a larger buy. I asked Davis how much he had. He stated he had 100,000 dollars in the trunk of his car and had over 900,000 dollars at his home. It sounded like a tall story but Davis was convincing and I half believed him.

He agreed to deliver a ten thousand dollar package to my hotel room. I went to the room and he went to a parking lot where his car was parked. He was observed by covering agents to take a package from the trunk and then proceed to the hotel. I admitted him to my room and after the delivery, he was placed under arrest. I was accused by the arresting officers of being wanted for a bank job up North. I immediately told the officers that the counterfeit money was owned by Davis, further that Davis had a load in his car and another load at his home. Davis did not appreciate my giving up on him, but eventually shrugged his shoulders and decided to cooperate with the officers. He took them to his car where 90,000 dollars was recovered; then to his home where he had stored under his bed almost a million dollars. Further questioning of Davis resulted in his identifying the printing shop where the notes were made. This shop was raided and the printer and several of his associates were arrested. When the last of the local arrests were made, I looked at my watch, shook my head and could not believe that the case only took about three hours to complete.

There is no doubt that the only reason this could have been wrapped up so swiftly was because a good citizen had the guts to come forward with the valuable information that he possessed. The counterfeit in this particular case was of excellent quality and had it been distributed in the proper manner, it would have tied up many investigators for a long period of time. The loss to the public could also have been great.

It appeared that I was returned to New York to face bank robbery charges, the defendants pleaded guilty and the informant had no problems with Davis or anyone else. This is the type of ending we all strive for, expecially when it involves the good citizen.

Inadvertent Informing

There is a type of an informant who is an unwitting informant. He is a man who has had several drinks, has some information and shoots his mouth off in a public place where it is overheard by another person, sometimes a police officer. This informant actually is giving information but unwittingly. This information

Figure 3. Exterior of print shop in midwest which printed several million dollars in counterfeit notes.

Figure 4. Author examines evidence after the seizure of plant (Fig. 14). The undercover work was completed and the premises were raided.

might be exaggerated but on closer scrutiny, it is generally learned that a percentage of it is true. If, during the evening, this person is identified and is later approached by an officer, he generally will give information but will pass from an unwitting informant into another category, depending upon what motivates him.

Repentance

There is a rare breed of informant called the repenter. This person is generally an older person who has spent many years in jail and was either double-crossed by his own associates or somewhere along the line "got religion."

I have in mind "Old Sol." Sol was released for the third time from Sing Sing Prison in New York over twenty years ago. He was a product of the East Side slums and all during his youth made his money by his wits. He was a burglar, a narcotic peddler and later became a "flopper."

Sol explained that a flopper was a man who had much training in falling. He would fall in front of an automobile that was just starting up. Two of his friends would be witnesses to the fact that the car knocked him down. A dishonest doctor and lawyer were part of the team who saw to it that the victim recovered a substantial sum from the insurance company.

There came a time when Sol's activities were brought to the attention of the District Attorney. Sol and his group were arrested. The group cautioned Sol to keep his mouth shut, which he did. Shortly thereafter, at a trial, all Sol's friends testified against him. They were given suspended sentences and Sol was sentenced to prison for 7½ to 15 years.

This was not the first experience that Sol had with friends who gave him up and after this experience, he became a repenter. He was genuinely sorry for all the crimes he had committed and he was against crime and criminals in every phase and form. I had occasion to interview Sol shortly after his release from prison and he impressed me with the fact that he was going straight and that in the event he had heard anything that was of interest to me, he would call me.

I have known Sol for so many years that I feel we are old

friends. Not many weeks pass before Sol is on the telephone and we get together for a sandwich and a bull session. One Christmas, I gave Sol a radio just for old times sake. It took hours of explaining before Sol was convinced that this was not a reward for anything he had done for me. To date Sol is responsible for making five good cases for the Government and the State.

This is another example of a case where an informant has to be handled very delicately inasmuch as this man had no other angle. We were careful never to expose him in any judicial proceedings. On one occasion, it was necessary to dismiss the case against two counterfeiters when it appeared that Sol would have to be called as a witness. Many investigators would pass Sol off as a mental case during the first interview. It would take a lot of experience to buy Sol's story that he would honestly help the police in a criminal matter and would not expect anything in return. He differs from the good citizen in that he is generally a man with a long criminal record and feels that informing is the best method to pay back the State or the Government the wrongs he has done in the past.

Eccentricity

Probably the hardest type of informant to deal with is the eccentric, the demented or the man who is known in the police jargon as the "psycho." Most officers feel that categorizing a man as a psycho is a good enough excuse to do nothing further on the case or the information he is supplying. This is definitely a wrong approach. There are many people who are classified as psychos who have good information and are good informants. True they are hard to handle but nevertheless they sometimes have excellent information and are willing to impart it.

Big Bill had just been released from a mental institution and returned to his old neighborhood. He was there but a short time when he learned that some of his old friends were engaged in a counterfeiting scheme.

For some unknown reason, he decided to report the matter to the local police. Unfortunately, the police knew he had just been released from a mental institution and did not pay any attention to him. In desperation, Big Bill went to the FBI and finally was directed to the Secret Service. I interviewed Big Bill and he told me that he had just been released from a State institution, having spent seven years there. At times during the interview, he appeared perfectly normal though at other times, he was obviously a psycho.

After questioning him for some time, it certainly appeared that he knew some of the violators that were involved in this counterfeiting ring. We looked far back into Big Bill's background and found that he had served many prison sentences and was in jail with some of the people he was informing on. Big Bill agreed to introduce an undercover agent to one of his friends.

I worked the case and I had no trouble in making a purchase of counterfeit notes after Big Bill gave me a big build-up. Shortly after the introduction, Big Bill tried to kill his wife and was returned to a mental institution. We felt that we had gone as far as we were able in investigating the case. We made several arrests on the strength of the purchases I had made and one of the defendants proved to be the printer. He worked for a fairly large printing outfit. He managed to get a key to the premises. On weekends, he would enter the shop and use their facilities to make the counterfeit money. The plates and negatives were found in his locker and the case was wrapped up in a very short time.

I hate to think of what might have happened if Big Bill would have called on the telephone in one of his less lucid moments. He could have easily been brushed off for the mental case that he was. All officers must take their information from wherever they can get it and run it out before deciding that they are wasting their time on a psycho or other type of mental case.

STOOL PIGEON

A phrase commonly used for an informant is a stool pigeon. Stool pigeons are a special category of informants. All stools are informants but all informants are not stools. A stool is generally a decoy to draw others into a net. However, he often plays the violators and police officers against one another. He gives information to both sides in an attempt to keep good relations with both the police and violators and tries to profit from both. This type of informant is very dangerous as he cannot be trusted and he is the type that may get an undercover agent injured if it suits his purpose.

Sometimes these professional stool pigeons have good information, other times they invent the information because it suits their particular purpose. It is very important for the undercover agent or the interviewing agent to recognize a stool pigeon immediately. Working a case with a stool pigeon is a difficult matter because very little information is given to him by the police while the case is progressing. Sometimes it is necessary to give the stool pigeon false information to see if he uses it against the police. The danger from professional stool pigeons is lessened if he is recognized and placed in the proper category in the beginning of the case.

Certain informants have to be tested in order to find out whether or not the information they are giving is genuine. In Secret Service work, it generally is not necessary to test the informant because the type of crime they have to investigate (counterfeiting) is unique. In most cases, the evidence disappears after it leaves the suspect's hands. In the case of narcotics, it is absorbed by the addict. In the case of illicit alcohol, it is disposed of by the consumer. However, in counterfeiting, the evidence is always returned to the government through banking sources. The Secret Service knows each day how much counterfeit money is being passed in every locality in the United States. If an informant says he was out with a group passing counterfeit notes in a certain area the previous week, these notes must come in to the local Secret Service office. In a short time, if the notes do not come in, it can be assumed that the informant is lying.

KEEPING THE BARGAIN

There comes a time in the interview with the police officer and the informant when the police officer has determined why the informant is giving the information. When this point is reached, the officer and his organization enter into another phase of the case, and that is meeting the price or the conditions that have been set either directly or indirectly by the informant. If the informant is motivated only by a reward and he is a professional, he will generally tell the officer exactly how much money he wants. Very often, it is too high and it becomes necessary for the officer or a representative of the department to come to a meeting of the minds with the informant.

There are many informants that believe that they should get a percentage of what is seized. Sometimes, this can be worked out with companies that have insured the stolen merchandise or with the agency for whom the seizure is being made. After some discussion with the informant, a price will be agreed upon and it is of the utmost importance that the officer and the agency live up to the terms of the bargain. No officer should agree to a price unless he is absolutely sure that his agency will, in fact, pay that much money and he definitely should have an approval from someone before he even proceeds with the case.

If an informant needs help in another criminal matter, it is desirous that inquiries be made to see if he can be helped, that is, a call to the district attorney who is handling his case to see if a reduced charge or a suspended sentence can be worked out. Here again, it is very important that the officer live up to the terms of the bargain he has made. A police department will soon get a bad reputation if they continually make promises to informants that they cannot or will not keep. Sometimes it is better for an officer to say "I can guarantee nothing but I will personally make a visit to the district attorney and discuss this with him and you will have to be guided by what he says." Most informants who need help will be satisfied if someone makes an effort in their behalf, while the results might not be what they expected, they will generally be satisfied.

It is also necessary for the officer to weigh what he expects to recover against what the informant wants. Very often, the informant will give a police officer a misdemeanor and expect the officer to help him with a felony. This could be explained very easily to the informant at the time of the interview.

Usually, it is a good idea to get the informant out of an official office. It is a good idea for the officer assigned to the informant to take him to lunch or go out and have a cup of coffee with him. It is during this time, that an officer can learn a lot about the informant without making it appear that he is questioning him.

WHO DOES THE INFORMANT BELONG TO?

An eternal question always arises in police business as to who the informant belongs to. This is a question, the answers to which could fill a book. Some police officers feel that an informant is their own personal property. They feel this way because in many agencies the police officer pays the informant out of his own pocket and is rewarded only by the possibility of a promotion after the informant makes some good cases for the police officer. I do not personally subscribe to this method. I do not believe that any police officer should have to pay for anything he does in the line of official business, much less pay the informant out of his pocket. But if this situation exists in a department, it is a logical assumption that the informant belongs to the officer. I believe an informant should belong to the organization but not to any individual. By the same line of thinking, the organization should have sufficient funds to pay the informant for the services he performs and no police officer should incur any personal expenses when he is dealing with an informant. In this way, the organization maintains control of the informant and merely assigns an individual police officer to work with him.

INFORMANT IDENTIFICATION

The informant should be designated by a number or code name. Somewhere in the department, the information on the informant should be kept in a confidential and locked receptacle and made known to officers on a "need-to-know" basis. In writing reports the informant should be referred to by his number or code name.

Sometimes in writing reports, it will suffice to say that information was obtained "from a confidential source." In the event it is necessary to produce these reports in court, no information will be given in the report which could identify the informant. All efforts should be made to keep the identity of the informant confidential. However, it is becoming more difficult to do this as defense counsels, under the *Jencks Decision,* are getting copies of the reports produced in court. Very often, judges will order a police officer to name his informant. Here, a decision has to be made whether or not to expose the informant or to refuse and have the case thrown out of court. Each case would have to be handled individually and judged on its own merits. Generally, the head of the unit would work this out with the District Attorney and it would be planned in advance whether to lose the case or expose the informant. It must be borne in mind that some informants do not care whether or not they are exposed. This is also worked out with the informant prior to any trial. The officer working with the informant will have already learned whether or not the informant has any objection to being named in court. Surprisingly, there are a good many informants who do not care whether or not their name is mentioned in court.

When working with an informant, the officer assigned to him should endeavor to get the informant's photograph and criminal record. I do not suggest that the informant should be sat down and photographed but, through conversations, an officer can learn if the informant has a record and then obtain his photograph. This photograph can be placed on the back of the informant's card that is locked in a confidential file. This would serve to identify an informant years later when perhaps the whole office personnel has been replaced due to normal attrition.

Sometimes an officer is asked to meet an informant after hours. If he has never met the informant before, the photograph in the file will help him identify the informant.

DEVELOPING INFORMANTS

Developing informants is the responsibility of everyone involved in police work; all the way from the supervisor to the newest recruit in the police department. Informants come to police departments in many ways. Sometimes, they walk into the office and announce that they have information to give, sometimes they call on the telephone. It is important that in either case, the person handling the informant do so in an intelligent manner.

Informants sometimes are strange breeds and handling them is an art. When a telephone call is received from an informant, the officer should try to arrange a meeting. In the beginning the informant is very wary of meeting a police officer and sometimes it takes a person with a lot of personality to have the informant agree to meet him. No police officer should dismiss a telephone call from an informant as a crank call. He should make every effort to attempt to meet the person and find out for sure whether or not it is a crank call. Sometimes, very important information comes over the phone and it is given by people who do not want to become involved. It is very easy for a police officer to dismiss the call as the work of a crank. We have discussed in an earlier chapter that even though a person may be a crank or psychopath, it is still possible that he can have information which could be used by the police. The only way to find out is to see the person and interview him personally.

Sometimes, an informant is referred by another agency. The agency generally will give an evaluation of the informant before the informant arrives. At this time, it is important to ask the other agency what the informant wants and why he is informing. The other agency will generally tell you exactly what the informant wants. It is important never to expose the identity of an informant, especially if he is given to you by another agency. This would certainly result in hard feelings, not only between the agents but also between the departments. In short, a conversation with the informant in the presence of a representative of the other agency is desirable. At this meeting, the ground rules can be laid and the representative of the other agency would know exactly what his informant is to get and what promises were made.

Very often informants do not realize the importance of the information they are giving and do not realize what can happen to them in the event they are exposed. The following is a good example.

Jim was a young man who worked for a local bank. This bank was in a run-down neighborhood in Queens, New York. Jim was a product of the neighborhood and knew everyone in it, both good and bad, as he spent his whole life in the one house. While Jim knew a lot of bad people, he kept himself clean and obtained a decent job at the bank.

One day Jim was approached by Kato. Kato was the leader of a band of thieves in the neighborhood and had access to many thousands of dollars in United States Treasury coupons. Kato asked Jim if he could filter the coupons through the local bank or perhaps find a buyer for the coupons. Kato promised Jim a cut of the profits if he was successful.

I interviewed Jim the next day when he decided to come to the office and report the matter. Jim was living with his widowed mother and was her sole support. He told me that he would be willing to do anything we suggested. He would even introduce an undercover agent to Kato. I knew the background of Kato. He was responsible for three murders and was a very dangerous character. I knew regardless of how the case was worked, Jim would find himself in the middle. He had no way to escape as he could not afford to move and we could not support him. I told Jim that we could not use his services but we would appreciate his giving us information on the activities of Kato and his crew whenever he was able.

It was hard for Jim to understand why we did not go ahead with the case at that time. As a matter of fact, the case against Kato was later made with great success through the efforts of an informant who was not as vulnerable as Jim.

Before Kato went away to serve a seven-year sentence, he became involved in another murder and it was after this particular crime that Jim came to the office and stated he fully realized why we did not use his services.

In analyzing the case, much thought went into what could happen to Jim in the event his services were used to effect an introduction to Kato. It always came out the same. Jim had to be exposed and he undoubtedly would be killed. The whole case revolved around him and at that time, it appeared it just was not worth the effort it would take to keep Jim alive.

COOPERATION BY THE INFORMANT

In dealing with the informant prior to the case, it must be learned how far the informant will go. In other words, would he be willing to introduce an undercover agent to the suspect. This would be the ideal condition as far as the agency is concerned because with an undercover agent working, the chances of success are highly probable. If the informant will not introduce an agent, will he make a purchase of the contraband by himself and be covered by agents? This is not a very desirable situation, for in order to make the arrest, the informant has to testify and his testimony would have to be corroborated by the covering agents. Sometimes informants, for their own particular reasons, desire this situation and are not concerned about the possibilities of being called as a witness. If he is willing to testify, then a successful case can be made. If the informant is not willing to do either of the above, then he usually will agree to give information from time to time. While this situation is highly desirable, it generally does not help too much in an undercover case. The important thing in any of the above situations is to find out from the informant if he is willing to testify at a trial and have his identity become known. It is of the utmost importance to find out how far the informant will go as the whole undercover case depends on it.

Sometimes it takes many interviews with the informant to find out how far he wants to go. Sometimes his fears are unfounded. Other times, he is sufficiently removed from the suspect; even if his identity does become known, no actual danger exists. Again, each case has to be handled as an individual case as no two are exactly alike. Many possibilities have to be explored with the informant until he sees a situation that suits both the agency and himself. This can only be done by discussing all the possibilities with the informant.

I recall a case where the informant knew a certain person had access to a large amount of counterfeit money. Only the informant and the suspect knew of its whereabouts. The inform- ant could not think of any situation where the government could seize this money without him being exposed. Many situations and possibilities were discussed and were turned down by the informant. Finally, out of desperation, I suggested that during the course of a routine investigation, I would stop at the suspect's house. I suggested that the informant would be at the house visiting the suspect at the time. I would make innocuous inquiries and then leave. The informant would tell the suspect that the visit was obviously a phony and he would suggest that the suspect change the location of the counterfeit money and to do it as quickly as possible as he felt the Secret Service was up to something. The suspect would be followed to the second hiding place and placed under arrest.

The informant listened to the above suggestions and to my complete surprise he stated that he thought it would work. He made a few changes and we went through with the plans. The amount of counterfeit money involved was over 100,000 dollars. The suspect did not want to be caught with it in his house, and took the informant's suggestion that it be moved. We followed him when he left his house with the contraband and placed him under arrest at the time that he was depositing it in a second hiding place. The suspect eventually pleaded guilty and the informant never was suspected of being involved.

It is interesting to note that it took over fourteen hours of talking with the informant before the above plan was agreed upon.

Even though some informants try to drive hard bargains, it does not mean that they will not listen to the problems that the investigators have. Sometimes, the informants ask for too much money, sometimes they ask the police to do something that is illegal or impossible. If the officer will take the time to explain to the informant step-by-step why his bargain is impossible, some informants will then remove the obstacles that make it impossible for the informant and the police to get together. It takes an experienced officer to handle informants and it would be well for the younger officer to observe, whenever possible, the methods used by the more experienced men.

After all the details are worked out with the informant, the officer should make sure that he lives up to his part of the bargain. He must contact his superior and any other person that is necessary in keeping his part of the bargain. If it becomes necessary because of fast-moving events to make certain promises to an informant, the officer should explain that the bargain is subject to a final decision by higher authority. The informant will appreciate this, especially if he can see that the officer cannot check with anyone because of the time element.

Some informants are unique and it is very difficult to put them in the proper category. "Jimmy C" was unique, to say the least, and to this day, his motive remains a mystery.

Jimmy called the office one night and an appointment was made to meet him. Jimmy had considerable counterfeiting information and some samples of counterfeit notes that were being passed around the mid-town area of New York City. He was agreeable to introducing an agent to the source of counterfeit notes and he appeared very anxious to help make a case.

Jimmy appeared to have plenty of money and there was no indication that profit was his motive. The agent handling Jimmy took him aside and went out for a cup of coffee. When they came back, the agent advised me that Jimmy C had a problem that he wanted us to help him with.

Jimmy stated that his driver's license had been revoked some time ago and that he had over two hundred parking tickets pending against him. Before he would proceed with the case, he wanted our okay that the tickets would be taken care of and his license restored. This was practically an impossibility, as two hundred tickets would have made him the king of the "scofflaws" and no judge would go along with our request. Nevertheless, the following day, I made inquiries and after searching all the records, I could find no indication that there were any parking tickets pending against Jimmy under his true name or any of the aliases he had used. Neither was there any record that he ever had his license revoked.

At this point, it was very easy to go ahead and work with Jimmy. Jimmy made four good cases for us and after the cases were made, I advised him to go to the Motor Vehicle Bureau and apply for a license. He did. He took the test, passed and was issued a valid license.

To this day, I cannot understand what happened to the so-called tickets and the revoked driver's license. Nevertheless, at the end of the case, we had satisfied an informant and what appeared to be a tremendous obstacle was, in fact, no obstacle at all. If Jimmy was a psycho, he was one of the rare ones that did not show it.

It is very important to know the complete background of the informant, whenever practical. There have been many cases where police organizations have used informants who were actually fugitives and were being sought for criminal offenses in other areas. This is very embarassing for the police department or agency using the informant. As a matter of fact, some agencies require that an informant submit his fingerprints and he is not utilized until such time as a return is received on his prints. I do not subscribe to this procedure, undoubtedly, it is a safe method; however, I can see where many informants would object to being fingerprinted and the waiting time in obtaining a return might jeopardize the case.

HANDLING INFORMANTS

Police officers should refrain from using the words "informer," "stool pigeon," "squealer," "rat," etc. I have seen cases where an informant was in a room and a police officer referred to another person as a stool or an informant. This, of course, did not set well with the informant who was in the room. Even though the officers are talking about someone else, the informant feels that he will be referred in the same manner when he is not there.

Over the years, I have used the word, "friend" especially in talking to an informant or referring to someone else who is giving information.

All possible information regarding criminal activities should be obtained from the informant when he is being interviewed. Very often, agencies will only question the informant on information that is of interest to their particular service. This is all wrong because very often an informant could have information about some very serious crimes and will not volunteer this information unless he is questioned about it. Obtaining information on a crime that is of interest to another service is one of the more important aspects of police work. The easy exchange of information between departments builds up confidence and trust in one another. In some instances, it is beneficial for departments to exchange informants when the informant has information for another jurisdiction. Not many people will subscribe to this but I have seen it work over the years with great success. The department who originally developed the informant can maintain a hold on him, even though the informant is cooperating with another agency.

Police officers and agents must learn to speak on the proper level with an informant. There are too many officers who look down upon informants and make it very obvious during the interview. There is nothing that will freeze the informant quicker than an interview with an officer who appears to be talking down to him. There are times when the informant obviously has more education than the police officer and it is important that an officer with more experience and education handle this type. Here you have a situation in reverse, where an informant talks down to a police officer because he feels superior to him. *The ideal situation is to have the informant and the officer speaking on the same level.*

In handling an informant, do not let him overestimate his importance. Informants should not be given a license to violate the law. This is a problem that many police departments are experiencing. There are some police officers who will allow informants to handle stolen property and sell it at a profit. They will then inform on their source, enabling the police to arrest the burglars or receivers. This usually develops into a situation where the informant feels he has a license to operate and he "gives the police crumbs while he keeps the whole loaf." Police officers should exert every effort to make it clear to the informant that he has no right to violate the law because he is working with the police.

Tommy was a "knock-around" guy who stumbled on some counterfeiting information. He was willing to give me this information for several hundred dollars. The information was certainly worth the price and we worked with Tommy in trying to make the case. In the midst of the case, Tommy stated he had to leave. I asked him why. He said he and two of his friends were going to stick-up a motel in a nearby town. Before I could talk him out of it, he left the office and did not return.

I called the State Police at the nearby town and they kept the motel covered over the weekend. Sure enough, at about 3:00 on a Sunday morning, Tommy and two of his friends attempted to hold up the motel and were apprehended by the troopers who were stationed inside at a vantage point.

I later had an opportunity to talk to Tommy at the local jail. He could not believe that I was the one who was responsible for his arrest. He stated that he felt as long as he was cooperating with the Federal authorities, we could at least give him a chance to make a living. Needless to say, he went away very bitter stating that the Secret Service had double-crossed him.

Keep in touch with informants, see them regularly. Informants are human beings and many of them are fine persons. Police and Federal officers are always anxious to obtain any information that they have. Sometimes, an informant gives information, he is paid, and no one ever sees him again. The informant perhaps does not come around to give information because he does not think that the particular agency whom he is familiar with can use the information. I have made it a practice over the years to visit informants who have been of service to me. It is surprising how pleased many of them are to have an agent call at their home or meet them somewhere just to pass some time with them over a cup of coffee or a sandwich. An informant sometimes can recall something which can be very useful to the Service, especially if the officer tells the informant it is more or less a social visit and that the officer has no motive other than to renew old acquaintances. This is very good for the informant's ego and he will double his efforts to be of assistance, especially if his previous experience with the agency has been favorable.

I had heard that an informant whom I had known for twenty years was ill at home. One night, I decided to go up and see him. I brought him a carton of his favorite cigarettes and spent an hour with him. It had been a very long time since he had given me any information and I was sure that he did not have any and I told him so.

Throughout the conversation in the evening, we had been talking about some of the "boys in the neighborhood." He brought me up-to-date on what each of them was doing and mentioned that one, Little Jack, was living in a rooming house nearby. The informant felt that Jack was on the "lam" but did not know who was looking for Little Jack. I told the informant that we were looking for Little Jack for the past year and had a warrant for him. The informant opened the window of his apartment and was able to point out the building where Little

Jack was. Needless to say, within two hours, Jack was apprehended. He could not understand how he was found, living in this remote neighborhood.

Use all legitimate means to develop informants. This is a never-ending task for all police officers. Informants are developed by having defendants cooperate; the police officer making friends with various people that he comes in contact with; sometimes relatives have information which is useful. There is a never-ending source for information as long as the police officer will take the time to try to develop the source.

An agent had arrested Manuel for stealing his brother-in-law's government check. Manuel's wife was pregnant and this case almost appeared as though it could be handled as a "family matter." When it was brought to the attention of the Assistant United States Attorney, it was decided to charge Manuel with forgery.

Manuel pleaded that his wife was alone at home; that he had no money for bail and that he would positively appear if he was released on his own recognizance. The agent was instrumental in having Manuel released. Manuel was very thankful and told the agent that someday he would like to repay the favor. For the want of something to say, the agent reminded Manuel that he was interested in counterfeiting in addition to check forgery. It appeared unlikely that a man of Manuel's stature would ever have any information on counterfeiting.

The following day, Manuel called the agent and told him that he knew of a friend that was printing something illegal in his cellar. A surveillance was maintained at the address mentioned and after five days, a complete counterfeiting plant was seized.

The counterfeits that were involved were five dollar and ten dollar bills that had been plaguing New York City for approximately seven months. Up to the time that Manuel gave his information, there was very little intelligence obtained on this plant, as it was a one-man affair and he only dealt with his own particular ethnic group.

It is obvious that this case was made because the agent had a little compassion for the defendant and went out of his way to see that the man was released on his own recognizance at a time when his wife needed him.

FORCING AN INTRODUCTION

In working an undercover case, very often an informant refuses to introduce an agent to the suspect. There are times when the agency knows all about the background of the suspect and feels sure that there is no danger to the informant, apparent or otherwise, if he does make an introduction. There does come a time when an agent has to force an introduction. Some informants are reluctant to introduce an agent because the suspect has stated that he did not want to meet any strangers.

Frank, a "knock around" kid from the east side, went into a local pizzeria for lunch every day. The owner of the pizzeria, though he had no criminal record, had many contacts in the underworld. There came a time when Sal, the owner of the pizzeria, made a connection to purchase narcotics and counterfeit money.

One day when Frank came into the pizzeria, Sal showed him sample ten dollar and twenty dollar counterfeit notes. He told Frank that he could get them in any quantity and was also able to obtain heroin and cocaine. Frank reported this offer to the Secret Service and I had occasion to interview him.

I asked Frank if he would take me into the pizzeria. He said absolutely no. Sal would not meet any strangers nor would he do business with anyone he did not know. I asked Frank if he was afraid of Sal and he said no but he was just positive that Sal would freeze up if a stranger came into the establishment. I tried many possibilities with Frank but he always came to the same conclusion that the plan would fail if someone other than himself attempted to purchase the counterfeits or narcotics. Finally, in desperation I said to Frank, "lets go up to the pizzeria and eat. Certainly, Sal cannot object to that."

At about 11:00 PM, Frank and I walked into the pizzeria and Sal greeted Frank with "didn't I tell you not bring any strangers into this place"? I immediately cut in and said, "look, I'm here to eat. This is a restaurant and I don't care if you talk to me or not." Frank and I sat at a table and ordered something to eat and drink.

About twenty minutes later, Sal came over to the table and stared at me for about two minutes, stuck out his hand and said, "my name is Sal. I can tell you're an okay guy. No hard feelings."

A short while later, I managed to have the informant, Frank, leave and I sat with Sal for a period of about an hour.

I told Sal I was "running" used cars up from Florida and would take anything down there that I could make a dollar on. Sal asked me if I ever handled junk. I told him I didn't know anything about it. He immediately gave me a ten minute discourse on the difference between cocaine and heroin, the difference in price and the proper method in testing the product to see if it was pure. He also showed me ten dollar and twenty dollar counterfeit bills and stated that I could purchase them in any amounts at fifteen dollars on the hundred. Unfortunately, this offer came at a time when both the Federal Narcotics Bureau and Secret Service were very low on funds and could not afford to invest any money in the case.

I ordered ten thousand dollars worth of counterfeit notes and an ounce of heroin. Sal told me to come back in an hour. I was able to leave, contact the covering agents and they were able to identify the person who made the delivery to the pizzeria and arrest him at the time the sale was made to me.

Sal pleaded guilty as well as the man who made the delivery to him. They were each given a penitentiary sentence. Sal hung himself shortly after he arrived at the Federal prison.

The informant, to this day is working in the same neighborhood. Apparently, no one suspected he was the informant in the case.

FEMALE INFORMANTS

Female informants are generally very good informants. Men confide in them and they usually have a great deal of information about the people they are associating with. Their motive is usually emotional and at the time they give the information, it is generally very reliable. They sometimes inform in order to seek revenge on a lover, husband or boy friend. Generally they inform because they have been jilted. At the time they decide to inform, it is necessary for the agency to proceed as rapidly as possible with the case. Very often they make up with their boy friend or husband and will not cooperate any further. As a matter of fact, they sometimes will go out of their way to spoil the case to prevent their loved one from going to jail.

Female informants present many problems and they should never be interviewed by only one agent. It is advisable to have two or more agents interview a female informant. If possible, the interview should take place at the office, in a restaurant or some public place in order to preclude the possibility of the informant making charges against the agents at a future date.

Most female informants do not have the best reputations in the world. Some are prostitutes and some like the idea of being involved in a police matter. Officers and agents again must be extremely careful about their relationships with these informants and they should not put themsleves in a position which could cause them to lose their jobs.

In general, it can be stated that female informants have reliable information, it must be worked on as quickly as possible. Everything said and accomplished should be documented as soon as possible.

Terry was a middle-aged woman who was happily married and had four children. There were no problems in her life until her sister, Molly, started to visit her. Molly had been in and out of trouble ever since she was a young teen-ager. She had run the gamut from truant to prostitute and finally confidant of some well-known gangsters in Brooklyn, New york.

One day, Terry came into the Secret Service office with probably the smallest piece of evidence that was ever used in police work. She had a three cent stamp and wanted to know if it was genuine. I examined the stamp and told her that it was a counterfeit. She stated that she suspected that it was and that there were perhaps a million of them around. I asked her where she got the stamp and she was reluctant to tell me. I told her she had some reason for coming to the Secret Service office and she should at least tell us the source of this particular stamp. She finally stated that she had a sister, Molly who was getting herself into some serious trouble. She thought that reporting this matter to the Secret Service would prevent her sister from getting involved in something even deeper than the counterfeiting of stamps.

She went on to say that her husband had a small stamp collection and that Molly brought him several of the counterfeit stamps that he could use. In subsequent conversations with her sister, Terry learned that her sister had access to a large amount of these stamps that were soon to be peddled on the street by a local group of narcotics peddlers.

I asked Terry if she would introduce me to her sister for the purpose of buying some of these stamps. She said that she could not, if something went wrong, she would be in serious trouble. After more discussion, it became apparent to me that Terry had another reason for informing. It appeared that she came home from work early one day and caught her sister in a compromising position with her husband. This was her real motive for informing.

After much more discussion, Terry agreed to tell Molly she knew a man who worked at the Post Office that was anxious to get some counterfeit stamps. She gave me Molly's telephone number and told Molly that if a man called "Nicky" telephoned, it would be her friend from the Post Office.

I called the number the following evening. A man answered. I asked if I could speak to Molly. He said, who is this, and I said Nicky. He said, Nicky from the Post Office and I said yes. He said, I know what you want to speak to Molly about. How can I get to see you. I told him that I would have a coffee break at about 10:00 and that he could meet me in front of the Post Office at 90 Church Street.

At the appointed time, I met Dom and we went to a local restaurant. He agreed to sell me counterfeit stamps at the rate of one dollar a sheet. The face value was three dollars. I told him that I could use two hundred sheets that night, but I could not pay for them until the following Monday. He agreed and stated that he would return in about an hour.

An hour later, I met him in the restaurant and this time he was accompanied by Molly. Molly immediately took charge of the conversation stating that the price offered by Dom was too low and actually I would have to spend $1.50 per sheet and I would have to purchase at least five hundred sheets. She proved to be a tough bargainer and it was necessary for me to agree to her terms.

Later that evening, Molly drove up in a car with Dom and

delivered five hundred sheets of stamps. She stated that if I did not meet her at her hotel the following Monday with the money, I would be in serious trouble.

The following Monday, I proceeded to the hotel and met Molly and several of her friends at the hotel. I paid her for the stamps and asked her if I could take another delivery. She agreed to give me three thousand sheets providing I could pay for them within four days. I agreed and followed three of her friends to a subway locker box where the stamps were turned over to me.

At that moment, I gave a signal to the covering agents and we were all arrested on the scene. Molly was arrested in her hotel room where she still had possession of the buy money.

All efforts on the part of "our" Service to get Molly to cooperate were unsuccessful. Her case was disposed of three or four months later in Federal court. She and her co-defendants were given five-year sentences. Molly would still not cooperate until she was in jail about a month and she saw no help forthcoming from the "higher ups" in the group. She sent messages to them but never received an answer.

Finally, one day she sent for me and I interviewed her at the prison. She stated that she was willing to tell the whole story and testify at the Grand Jury and at a trial against the people she was doing business with. She stated that she could also get her co-defendants to cooperate if she had an opportunity to talk to them. This opportunity was afforded her.

The matter was placed before the Grand Jury and resulted in fifteen indictments against her connections who were not only handling stamps but narcotics and counterfeit money. All the defendants were arrested and none of them saw fit to cooperate. Two of the defendants could not make bail, which was very high. They felt sure that they would receive help from the higher ups in the counterfeiting scheme. Again, no help was forthcoming.

At about this time, I received a telephone call from a woman who said she was Irving's wife. Irving could not make bail and he wanted to cooperate with the Government but did not want to be interviewed at the jail. Arrangements were made to have him brought to a place where he could be interviewed.

Irving was a veteran of World War II. He was allowed to join the

Army while serving a long prison term for armed robbery. He was given a release under the condition that he join the Army. Irving spent five years in the Army and won every medal except the Congressional Medal of Honor. He had one of the finest war records I had ever seen.

After getting his discharge, he went right back to peddling stolen property, narcotics, counterfeit money, etc. Irving stated that he would be willing to testify against the higher echelon in this case, if his bail could be reduced. He stated that he wanted to "hit the street" because his daughter was going to the hospital for a serious operation and he wanted to be near her. I asked him if he feared for his life? He stated that he feared no man in this world and that he could handle anyone that attempted to do him bodily harm. Arrangements were made to have his bail reduced. He was released and eventually testified before the Grand Jury.

Tony, the other man who could not make bail, was the only other person we had who could corroborate the information given by Irving. Tony contacted me and stated that his sister was being married and he desperately wanted to attend the wedding. Further questioning of Tony proved that he was the witness we needed to make the case complete against the manufacturers of the stamps and the principal distributors. Arrangements were made for Tony to attend the wedding. Tony testified before the Grand Jury.

While working on this case, important information had been developed to indicate that a commercial bank check was being made by the same group and they were "passing" about fifty thousand dollars to sixty thousand dollars of these checks every week. As a result of the cooperation of Irving and Tony, the manufacturers of the stamps, the counterfeit notes and the commercial checks were identified and arrested.

The investigations of the bank checks were given to another agency who were successful in arresting thirty-one persons, together with our twenty-eight arrests made it one of the larger conspiracies ever developed in the New York district. All of this emanated from the three cent stamp brought in by the informant, Terry, because she feared losing her husband to her sister.

It might be interesting to note that one of the defendants in this case attempted to sell the information on the entire counterfeiting scheme to the bank in question. This person contacted one of the security men at the bank who did not believe that anyone would actually counterfeit their paper. He did not attempt to ask the man's name and address and had no way of contacting this person when the checks began to show on the street. This is a good example of how an inexperienced agent can lose a case even before it starts. Had someone seen the necessity to negotiate with the informant, the bank could probably have saved hundreds of thousands of dollars. Everyone in the above case was sent to prison except three who disappeared, forfeited their bail and who have undoubtedly been murdered.

THE BON-VIVANT

Another rare type of informant is the one that does not care. He has been informing for a number of years. He takes a philosophical attitude about his work and does not particularly care whether or not he is exposed. As a matter of fact, this type of informant will take the stand if he is called, he will testify and generally make an excellent witness. He is a supreme egotist and will make cases for the sake of showing that he can do it.

Chris was exactly this type of informant. I met him quite a few years before. At the time, he was doing very well. He stayed at the best hotels and moved in the top circles. He could easily make a good living legitimately. However, he chose to stay in the gray and black area. He was the type that liked to report to just one person and he would go out of his way to help make a case. If he was doing well financially, he would not look for any remuneration. There were times where he spent a considerable amount of his own money to make the case.

He was meticulous, neat and well spoken and generally got along on his personality. Most people who dealt with him knew he was an informant but for some unknown reason, they took a chance with him, hoping that this one time he was playing it straight and not bringing in the police.

One day he came to me because he needed some help with another agency. I interceded for him and obtained the desired results. Before long he had made some friends with the other agency and was doing a lot of work for them.

On one occasion, he was out of town purchasing a load of stolen stocks and bonds. He was working closely with the authorities. Due to no fault of his own, the securities were delivered to Chris prematurely in his hotel room. Chris took the securities and told the person to leave the room, that he was not getting paid and that the police would arrive on the scene momentarily to take the whole bundle of securities. The person making the delivery went back to his connection who was waiting in the lobby and told him what had happened. Jack, the connection, became enraged and proceeded to Chris' hotel room. Chris would not let him in. Jack swore he was going to kill Chris and immediately began to kick the door down. When it was apparent that the door was coming down, Chris calmly got a revolver and fired a shot through the door. The bullet struck Jack in the head, killing him instantly. Shortly thereafter, Chris was arrested for homicide.

I had arrived in the same town about three days after Chris' arrest. While there was no doubt that he would win the case, he still needed a little help, someone to speak to the judge and mention that he had been working for various agencies in the past and the fact that he was reliable.

I went to the jail to see Chris. I had expected to find him "down in the dumps." True to form, he was in a squad room talking with a group of detectives. When I came in, he asked to be excused and we were shown into an anteroom where he could have a little privacy. I told him what I was planning to do and said I would see him in court the following day.

A short time later, a detective was showing me out of the jail and mentioned to me that Chris was a great guy. I asked him what he meant. He stated that his squad was preparing a raid on a large house of prostitution that was giving them trouble. It was a "must" that these premises be raided in the following eight or ten hours. Somehow, Chris got wind of the impending raid while he was in jail. He asked to see the man in charge. Chris told him that they were "barking up the wrong tree" because the house had been moved a week ago. He then gave them the true address of the house. The raid was made and was extremely successful.

Needless to say, Chris was treated royally during his short stay at the jail.

A few months after the shooting, Chris returned to New York. He told me that several of his friends were distributing counterfeit money. He said he would try to get them to stop, as he did not want to see them get arrested. He explained that they were semi-legitimate businessmen and merely peddled counterfeit money as a sideline. I told Chris that his feeling for his friends did not particularly interest me. If they were selling counterfeit money, I wanted him to introduce me to them and try to make a purchase. Chris objected for a while but later told me that he would see what he could do.

By this time, he was no longer "Dapper Chris," because of the shooting out of town he was now referred to as "Killer Chris" and was feared by many people in the underworld. Why they continued to do business with him remains a mystery.

One day, Chris called me and told me that he had an appointment with his two friends at a dining room in a swank New York hotel. I told Chris that I would go to the hotel merely to get a spot on his friends so that we would know them for future reference. Chris met his friends in the dining room as he had planned. At this point, I decided that this would perhaps be the ideal time to force an introduction. I had several agents in the vicinity covering me and I walked over to the table where Chris and his friends were seated. I shook hands with Chris and acted as though we were old friends. Chris had no alternative but to introduce me to his friends. They were introduced as Moe and Joe. There was no doubt they were businessmen. The conversation for the next hour was buy and sell, buy and sell. If they were involved in counterfeiting, they certainly were the most unlikely counterfeitors that I ever met.

Chris had to make some telephone calls and excused himself and left me with the "twins" as they became known to us. Moe asked me what I did for a living. I gave him the stock answer of "I buy and sell." He said, "buy and sell what?" I said, "anything." He looked at his partner and then reached into his inside pocket and pulled out a twenty dollar bill. He showed it to me; it was a counterfeit. He asked me if I liked it. I said I always liked twenty dollar bills. He said he could get me all I wanted at a discount. I asked why a discount and he said that they were bad ones. I asked him how much and he said twenty cents on the dollar in amounts of twenty-five thousand dollars. We bargained for a while and it was agreed they would sell me fifty thousand dollars in counterfeit notes for 7,500 dollars in genuine money. Moe said it would take two or three hours to get the stuff. I said it would take about an hour and a half for me to get my money. Either way, we agreed to meet back at the dining room in two hours.

When Chris returned to the table, Moe and Joe told him we had just concluded plans for a delivery of counterfeit notes. They asked Chris if I was all right. Chris said I could be trusted. Joe asked Chris not to set them up. Chris laughed and said he would never do anything like that. We parted company, and Chris and I left together. He said he should be angry because of the way I operated but he could not forgive Moe and Joe for being so hungry and trying to make a sale when he was not around. I asked Chris to lose himself for the rest of the afternoon, at least until the deal was made. He insisted on being there and so he joined me later when I again met Moe and Joe.

Joe stated they were ready to do business and asked me for my 7,500 dollars. I showed them a package of money and told them that I would pay them as soon as the counterfeits were delivered. Moe insisted that I pay them in advance. I said no, that the money was not mine and I could not gamble with other people's money. They then asked me to put up half the money to show good will. I again refused. We carried on this way for about an hour. Finally, Joe made a few telephone calls and asked me to wait until he returned. He stated he would be gone for an hour. He left and returned in an hour.

He took a small package from his pocket and asked me to open it. I did and the box contained two beautiful diamonds. He then showed me a memo slip from a jeweler in the neighborhood. This slip indicated the diamonds were worth five thousand dollars each and Joe had received them "on memo" from the jeweler. Joe told me to hold the diamonds and give him five thousand dollars so he could get the counterfeits delivered. I told him that I was not in the jewelry business and could not tell whether the diamonds were real or phony. Moe and Joe, having seen my money, were becoming quite frustrated as they knew they could not get the counterfeits without paying for them in advance.

Finally, Joe made a telephone call. A few minutes later he met a man and had a guarded conversation with him. The covering agents saw this and followed the man to New Jersey. Joe returned and told me that he gave the unknown man the two diamonds as collateral on the counterfeit note deal and he expected to get delivery in an hour or so.

The unknown man was seen contacting a known distributor in New Jersey and getting a package delivered to his car. The car returned to New York and the man came into the dining room of the hotel. He contacted Joe. I then suggested that we all go to a room that I had in the hotel.

On our way out of the restaurant, we were all arrested and brought to the room. Moe and Joe insisted that they were itinerant jewelers. I insisted I was a businessman. The police wanted to know what I was doing with the large amount of money in my pocket. The unknown man, called Tom, found it very hard to explain where he got the package of counterfeit money that was in his possession. Chris pleaded that he was an innocent victim of the whole affair.

The connection in New Jersey was picked up later in the day and the case was tied up in a nice little package. Chris later arranged bail for Moe and Joe and the whole deal did not mar their friendship in the least.

This is one of the imponderables of the police business.

In conclusion, it would appear that handling informants is an art that all officers must learn. To be successful in handling informants, an agency and its employees must have the respect and the confidence of the informants that they meet through various sources. The agency must live up to its commitments and every effort should be used to prevent the informant from being exposed, keeping in mind that informants like Chris are rare.

Chapter 2

THE SUSPECT
OBTAINING BACKGROUND

POLICE organizations which are endeavoring to work undercover cases must get all the information possible on the suspect. The quickest and the best source of information is the informant, especially if the informant is in a position to introduce a police officer to the suspect. If he makes an introduction, he generally has known the suspect for a long period of time. He could give the agency background information on the suspect and answer most questions that are put to him by the police. Some of the questions that have to be answered are the following:

1. How long has the informant known the suspect?
2. How well does he know him?
3. Does the suspect have any background or record with the agency that is investigating him?
4. Is the suspect capable of doing what the informant believes?
5. Is the suspect one of the top men or is he a "bag man or delivery boy"?
6. Can the undercover agent safely work where the suspect and his friends are likely to be?

These are important questions to be answered because in assigning an undercover agent to work with an informant, it is necessary to know the locale and most of the people involved so the undercover agent will not encounter a man he has previously roped.

1. Does the informant know who is behind the suspect?
2. How is the informant involved with the suspect?
3. Does one outclass the other?

Of course, many of the above questions are automatically answered when the suspect has a previous record with the agency. In the event that the suspect is new to the service or agency, the time must be found to answer the above questions before the case proceeds. These questions, if answered properly, will let the supervisor know the method he must use to protect the informant, what agent or agents he must use for the undercover work, what places must be covered during the operation and the identity of the people that might appear on the scene at the time of the "buy." In considering the suspect, it is beneficial to know what his habits are — what time he gets up in the morning, what time he leaves the house, what route he takes, the car he drives, the people he meets and where he spends his time. Is he a good family man? Does he spend his nights at home? Does he have children, what are their ages and what school do they attend? Will he be the type of man to keep contraband at home? Does he have a girl friend? Does he have another address, a sort of "home away from home"? Does he "front" for any business? Does he have a legitimate income? Knowing the answers to these questions in advance will make the undercover case easier to work and perhaps achieve more successful results.

There was a time when two agencies had warrants for a suspect. There was something in the suspect's background that indicated he might be armed. Much thought was given as to where the suspect should be arrested. At first it appeared that the best place to arrest him was at a club where he spent much time. It was finally decided to arrest him at his home.

A background check on this individual revealed that he had six small children living at home. It was decided that the suspect would not become involved in a gun battle which would jeopardize his wife and children. Elaborate plans were made by the two agencies to insure there would be no violence. The arrest at his home went very smoothly and although he had a small arsenal at his home, he made no attempt to use it. It was understandable; although he was a very vicious man, he still did not want to do anything that would jeopardize his children.

In investigating the background of the suspect, look for evidence that will fit in with the particular crime that is being investigated. Were his previous violations the same as the one he is being investigated for? Is there any indication that he might cooperate? Does his past record show any indication of a lesser sentence than his co-defendants? Does he have the reputation of being a "stand-up guy"? Does the informant's past experience with the suspect indicate that the suspect is reliable? In previous dealings with the suspect did the informant give money in advance or was it a hand-to-hand delivery? What is the suspects financial situation? Has he had recent arrests that required money for bail and lawyer's fees?

It is very important to know the suspect's financial condition because when he needs money badly, he may "throw caution to the winds" and take chances that he normally would not take. Most of the answers to the questions needed to appraise the suspect can be found in probation or parole records, reports from other agencies and of course, reports from the department who is making the investigation. Before attempting to work an undercover case, no detail, however slight, should be overlooked. By investigating the suspect, it will be easier for the agency involved to anticipate his moves. Very often, if enough is known about the supsect, many of his movements can be discounted as routine and much of the shadowing could be curtailed in order to minimize suspicion.

SUSPECTS PROBLEMS

In working an undercover case where contraband is involved, the agency and the undercover personnel should be aware that the suspect may be having trouble in "making things click" regarding the time of delivery. Patience has to be exercised. Several hours can make the difference between success and failure. The suspect generally is not truthful in telling why the delivery is taking so long. At times, he is embarrassed to admit that he is getting the merchandise third or fourth-hand and has to wait until the other people involved are ready to make the delivery. Sometimes twelve or fourteen hours are not too long to wait for a delivery. As long as the suspect indicates that he is expecting the merchandise, the undercover personnel and covering agents should wait.

I can recall a case where an undercover agent was expecting a delivery of 100,000 dollars in counterfeit money at a local diner. Originally the suspect stated that he controlled the plant and the merchandise leaving the plant. He tried to make the undercover agent believe that the operation was entirely his.

When the time came for delivery, the suspect had to wait for another man to come home from work and the other man had to wait for someone else to take the money from its hiding place. The covering agents in this particular case became very impatient with the delay and several times during the operation they called me and indicated that they did not believe a delivery would be made. Each time I contacted the undercover agent he felt that a delivery would be made but might take longer than anticipated. A delivery came fourteen hours after it was expected. The suspect had to get some money in advance before a delivery would be made to him. The extra hours that we waited in this case made the difference between success and failure.

SALESMANSHIP

In most cases, the suspect will try to impress the undercover agent that he is "Mr. Big." He will try to show that he controls the entire operation and that he does not have to answer to anyone. In most cases the undercover agent knows that this is not true. Nothing would be accomplished by "knocking" down this claim. The suspect is a salesman and bragging is a part of his "stock and trade." Very often, the undercover agent should go along with this type of suspect. It is good for the suspect's ego and will establish a good relationship between the undercover agent and the suspect. This also tends to make a successful case.

STEREOTYPE OPERATION BY SUSPECT

Some suspects, either by "force of habit" or suspicion, have a certain way they want to conduct business. It is very difficult to get them to change their methods. These traits are usually found in the older suspects who have found that they have been successful in distributing contraband in a way that protects them from being set up. Attempting to "make a buy" from this type of suspect is very difficult because he will usually want the money in advance and he might not even be on the scene when the delivery is made.

Tony lived in a mid-western city. He had been in this country for over twenty-five years. He had established several successful businesses and was also a member of an organized group who had terrorized this particular city for quite a few years. Tony made a lot of money legitimately and made a lot more illegitimately. He was involved in smuggling aliens across the border, handling narcotics and also a "numbers" bank. There came a time when he became the principal distributor of a new counterfeit note that appeared in the mid-west. Tony was very careful about who he conducted business with and because he was successful, he would not change his method of delivery. The particular counterfeit note that he was handling was getting very wide distribution and the passers were quite successful in victimizing the public.

An informant had purchased some counterfeit notes from Tony. Tony confided in the informant that he had over a million dollars worth of these counterfeits and he was anxious to dispose of the whole lot. The informant reported this to the Secret Service and a decision was made to send an agent with the informant to attempt to make a purchase of counterfeit notes. This particular agent happened to be my brother Bob Motto.

Tony had a pizzeria, a large supermarket and a bar and grill all in one building. This building had a large basement where Tony stored soda, groceries and everything else needed in connection with his business. This, we suspected was also the storage place for the large amount of counterfeit notes we felt that Tony possessed.

Four weeks later, the informant introduced my brother Bob to Tony. Tony was very suspicious and immediately accused the informant of bringing the law into his place of business. This was another quirk that Tony had. Every time he met a stranger, he would accuse the stranger of being a "cop" and would threaten the informant with death if anything happened to convince him that the stranger was a "cop."

After two or three meetings, Tony "warmed up" to my brother and their meetings ended when Tony delivered fifty thousand dollars to Bob. No arrest was made as a result of this buy. It was agreed that this buy would never be used because the informant introduced Bob to Tony. It was decided that Bob would bring another agent in and attempt to acquire the million dollars in counterfeit notes. The arrest would be made at that time. As much

"heat" as possible would be thrown on the second agent to make it appear as though he was the informant in the case.

About three weeks after the first buy, it was decided that I would accompany my brother, Bob, to this city and he would introduce me to Tony. He would tell Tony that I was a bank robber and that as a result of a recent robbery, I had enough money to purchase all the counterfeit notes that Tony had left.

On a Saturday afternoon, both of us went into Tony's bar. Tony spoke broken English and very poor Italian, communicating with him was very difficult. As soon as the introductions were made at the bar, Tony called Bob aside and accused him of bringing a "cop" on the premises. He stated that he would not say anything in front of this stranger because he did not feel comfortable with him around. Bob and I sat at a table and had lunch. Shortly thereafter, Tony joined us. His first remark was that we looked like brothers. This was very disturbing because we did not want to give this impression to Tony. The conversation at the table was very cool and nothing was accomplished. We told Tony we would be back for supper later that evening.

It did not appear to me that anything could be done with Tony because of his attitude but Bob said that this was exactly the same attitude that Tony had of him at their first meeting.

Later Saturday night, we went back into the restaurant. Again, Tony joined us at the table. This time, for some unknown reason, he decided not to talk to Bob and directed his conversation toward me. He said he knew what I was there for and he was in a position to deliver a million dollars, providing I could give him 100,000 dollars in cash before the delivery. I told Tony that I had come into the city with 100,000 dollars and there would be no trouble making a purchase, providing the method of delivery was satisfactory. After discussing several methods of delivery, Tony said that he had one last method of making a delivery and this would be the only way he would handle it. He suggested that we come back to the bar at midnight with the 100,000 dollars in genuine currency. We would all proceed to the cellar under his bar. Immediately after the bar closed, he would count the 100,000 dollars that I had brought with me and he would let me examine and count the million dollars that he would arrange to have in the cellar.

He suggested that my brother and I be armed because he would have several people there who would also be armed to protect his counterfeit money. Tony stated that after the money was counted, we would remain several hours in the cellar until daylight. At this time, we would go into his grocery store, put the counterfeit notes in grocery shopping bags, walk out of the store, put the bags in the trunk of our car and be on our way. I told Tony that I liked this idea very much except I did not want to spend the whole night in his cellar because I had more important things to do. I suggested that I drive up to his store on Sunday morning and bring the 100,000 dollars with me. We would then go down to the cellar and it would take Tony a short time to count my money. I would take the counterfeit money and assume there was a million dollars there, put the money in shopping bags and leave as suggested by Tony. I reminded him that I would be back if there were any shortages. Tony thought this over for quite a while and then agreed to it. He suggested that we be in front of his grocery store at 7:00 sharp on Sunday morning. He stated that he would be in the store sweeping it. As soon as we pulled up, he would open the door and allow us to enter. He would examine my money immediately and then take us to where the counterfeit money was. I told him that these arrangements would be very good.

He again suggested that we be armed when we came, for our own protection. We left the premises and had a meeting at the office that night to make arrangements for the "buy" the next morning.

There still were many problems in trying to make the "buy" the way Tony suggested. If we were not using the first "buy" as evidence, we would have to see counterfeit money on Tony's premises before an arrest could be made. Tony wanted to see our money before we saw the counterfeits and this was the problem. We considered the possibilities for several hours and finally I decided that it would be done in the following way. As suggested by Tony, I would drive up across the street from his shop. My brother would get out of the car and I would stay in it. Bob would cross the street and we were sure that Tony would open the door as soon as he saw Bob and would ask him what was wrong. Bob would say, "my friend is very nervous because of all the talk about carrying guns. We are only two and we do not know how many people you have hidden on the premises. He is afraid that we will be stuck up as soon as we enter the store with the money." This is exactly what we did.

When Bob arrived at the store, Tony started screaming, "why doesn't your friend come in." Bob stated that his friend was scared to death and felt that Tony had many people on the premises ready to take his 100,000 dollars. Just as we planned, Tony said, okay, you can go down the cellar and look for yourself. Bob went down to the cellar and was supposedly looking for men who might "pull a hold up." Tony had two men in the cellar who were armed and there was several cartons which contained counterfeit money, right where the men were sitting. This was enough to give us probable cause for an arrest. Again, as we planned it, Bob came out of the store and yelled to me that everything was okay. "Get your money and come on in." We had made sure that on that Sunday morning there would be no cars strange to Tony on the street because Tony undoubtedly had friends checking the neighborhood. We had a surveillance truck equipped with a radio several blocks away where the agents and detectives inside had a clear view of my car. I had made arrangements with all concerned that as soon as I opened the trunk of my car, everything was set for an arrest.

When Bob told me that everything was okay, I left the car and opened the trunk and wasted some time attempting to take a briefcase out from the back of the trunk. This signal was seen by the men in the surveillance truck and a message went out to all cars to effect an arrest immediately. In about thirty seconds, four or five cars converged on the scene. Men got out with rifles, shotguns, etc. Tony and his group were completely overwhelmed. The counterfeit money was seized from the cellar along with some firearms and other contraband that Tony was dealing in.

Tony and his friends were later sentenced to ten years imprisonment. Tony had been successful most of his life in making deals the safe way. However, even with a man like Tony, arrangements could be made to make Tony deviate from his own method of operation. I doubt if Tony was even aware of the fact

Figure 5. Author examines a million-dollar seizure after a successful undercover case.

that he had changed radically from the safe position that he took in the beginning.

USING CONVERSATION FOR CORROBORATION

No undercover agent should underestimate any phase of the case he is working on. The case conceivably could end at any time during the negotiations and a successful case can still be made. One sample can be sufficient to convict a distributor in a counterfeiting case. Even a short conversation with the suspect about a previous sale can corroborate the testimony of another witness and result in the conviction of the suspect. Many counterfeit note distributors have been sent to jail for comparatively long terms on the strength of one or two sample notes given to an undercover agent. It should be borne in mind that a conviction, even on a one-note pass, carries a maximum sentence of fifteen years.

One of the toughest little men that I ever worked on was a man we will call Mario. Mario was no more than 5 feet, 2 inches tall and weighed 185 pounds. He drove a large trailer truck and was feared by all the men he dealt with. Mario was a hard-working man but as a sideline he also handled narcotics and counterfeit money. He operated successfully for quite a few years and was known for his shrewdness in handling deals. If he had the slightest suspicion that something was wrong, he would not gamble but would postpone the delivery indefinitely, if necessary, until he could test the purchaser and convince himself that the man was not a police officer.

Mario, in his youth, had spent quite a few years in jail as a result of atrocious assaults he committed on persons whom he suspected of double-dealing him. Mario always carried some sort of weapon he could use for these assaults. He was, however, careful not to carry the usual gun or knife. He learned at an early age that there were plenty of other weapons that could be used to assault people without taking unnecessary chances of being arrested for concealed weapons.

I was introduced to Mario by another suspect who did not know my identity. After two or three meetings with Mario, he told me he could get me counterfeit money in unlimited quantities. I asked Mario for a sample note and he said he would have one for me the following night. He then asked me to join him in a nearby tavern for a drink. It was necessary to ride to this tavern and Mario took this opportunity to see if he was being tailed. After driving three or four blocks, Mario called my attention to a car that was obviously following us. He tested this car for about a mile and there was no doubt in Mario's mind that they were interested in him. Mario's only problem was that he was not sure whether they were federal officers or local police. We finally arrived at the tavern and after a drink, I left Mario and made a telephone call to my office and advised them to discontinue the tail on Mario, because he was aware he was being followed. The surveillance car was immediately notified by radio to discontinue.

Mario again asked me to join him for a ride after we left the tavern. Mario tested for over an hour but could not find a tail and was convinced that perhaps it was the local police.

I met Mario the following night. Mario stated that he did not have the sample as he was still testing for tails. It took two more weeks before he would even talk about samples again. Finally, there came a time when Mario was convinced that he was no longer being tailed and he agreed to deliver the samples to me on a subsequent night. I kept the appointment but Mario did not show up. I waited for several hours and when it became apparent that something went wrong, I discontinued. When I returned to the office, I learned that Mario was arrested in a small nearby town when he tried to buy a drink with a counterfeit twenty dollar bill. The police held him for our Service and it was decided to arraign Mario on the charge of passing one counterfeit bill. Mario pleaded not guilty and claimed he was an innocent victim, that he had received the counterfeit twenty dollars when he cashed his paycheck. Mario made bail and was released.

A few nights later, I met Mario again and he told me of his troubles. He told me on the night he was arrested he had the sample counterfeit for me and stopped in a local bar for a drink. He stated that after several drinks, he inadvertently gave the sample note to the bartender. He stated that he had discussed this matter with his lawyer who told him that the government did not have a case and probably would not prosecute on a one-note pass. Mario told me that he was not going to handle any more counterfeit notes until his case was disposed of.

Not long afterward, his case came up for trial. Testimony was given by the bartender about the note that Mario had passed. Throughout the proceedings, Mario kept calm and he was sure that the jury would not convict him. I was then called in as the last Government witness. This was quite a shock to Mario. When I took the stand, Mario "blew his top." He shouted obscenities at me and the whole judicial system. He had to be restrained during my testimony. I carefully went through our whole relationship and the conversation we had prior to his arrest and how I waited three hours for a sample on the night he was arrested. His lawyer made a feeble attempt at a defense which was not too impressive. The jury was out only fifteen minutes at which time they returned a verdict of guilty. Mario was sentenced to seven years. After the sentencing, he threatened the judge, the assistant United States Attorney and myself. However, Mario served his time, the threats never materialized and upon his release, Mario slipped into obscurity.

I doubt if Mario would have received any more time even if he had made a sizeable delivery of notes. The pass, together with the conversation we had, was enough to convince the judge and jury that Mario was not an innocent victim of a counterfeit note.

HANDLING THE SUSPECT AFTER ARREST

Unfortunately, there are some investigators who feel that an undercover case ends with the arrest of the distributors after the delivery of the contraband. Undercover work is a means to get to the source of the crime. There are times when many undercover cases must be worked in order to get to the source or to "the plant" as it is known in a counterfeiting case. When the suspect is arrested, the arresting officers must use knowledge and psychology in attempting to get the suspect to name his source or to assist in locating the plant. Most people who are arrested in the act of committing a crime go into something that resembles shock, especially if it is their first arrest. The knowledgeable officer can turn this "state of shock" into an advantage. If he can question the suspect properly, gain his confidence and show the suspect the advantages of cooperating, the defendant very often will cooperate and bring the case to a successful conclusion. I have seen many sources "slip through the fingers" of incompetent investigators because they did not handle the defendant properly, immediately following the arrest. They had lost sight of the fact that the arrest was the beginning of another phase of the case. They had made the mistake of playing the role of the tough cop and trying to bully admissions from the defendant. They had completely disregarded the fact that the defendant has certain rights which can never be denied him. Explaining one's rights is jealously guarded by the Constitution and the defendants expect to be advised, even though these rights have been brought to their attention by the press, radio, television, etc.

An arrest causes many problems for the person arrested. Criminals do not expect to be arrested when they are in the act of committing a crime and they generally do not make plans accordingly. There are times when these problems are just as important to the defendant as the arrest itself. The wife has to be notified, a date may be waiting at some rendezvous, the children have to be brought to school, or the mother might become seriously ill if not notified properly. The intelligent officer will listen to these problems and make an attempt to solve them, if at all possible, and if it does not violate any departmental rules. A genuine interest in these problems will establish a rapport between the defendant and the officer. It is important to note that there is no safety in numbers when questioning a defendant. Suspects, witnesses and defendants are reluctant to talk before a group. They feel they can always deny a statement made before just one officer. It should also be borne in mind that most defendants do not think too kindly of an officer who takes out a pencil at the very start of an interview and attempts to record every word. Immediately after an arrest, many defendants appreciate a cigarette, cup of coffee and a man-to-man conversation with the arresting officer. This sometimes brings far more success than a combination of out-dated police methods.

Figure 6. Home in suburbs where large counterfeit plant was seized.

Everett and his family were quite popular in their community. They had moved to a sleepy New England village and were immediately accepted by the usually suspicious inhabitants. Ev had a million dollar personality. His wife was a former professional ballet dancer who lost no time in establishing ballet classes for the children in the community. Their own children were extremely popular with the other school children in the town. Ev and his wife had bought a refurbished mansion where they lived and where Ev ran a publishing company. Ev was extended all kinds of credit, especially when he made it known that he was related to a very high government official (which was not true. However, he did have exactly the same name as a Cabinet member.)

Several months later, there appeared in the larger cities in the area, a number of counterfeit ten dollar and twenty dollar notes and some counterfeit American Telephone and Telegraph stock certificates. At this time, there was nothing suspicious about Ev except the people of the community thought Ev was working very hard "burning the midnight oil" in the basement of his home. They knew he had financial problems and felt he was working overtime to meet his debts.

One day, an informant came into our office and told us that he had been offered counterfeit tens and twenties by a man named Harvey who ran an auto repair shop in one of the nearby cities. The informant was just another customer in this shop and he had no close ties with Harvey. The informant stated that he would have no objection to introducing an agent to Harvey.

I accompanied the informant to Harvey's shop. After a conversation lasting about a half hour, Harvey asked me if I would be interested in purchasing some "funny money." I told him that I did not know too much about it but I would take a few hundred dollars and see how it went. I would also show the money to some friends and try to get some large orders. Harvey was able to supply me with several hundred dollars worth immediately, and told me that he could get me the notes in any amounts as long as I gave him a few days notice. The notes that he gave me were examined and they were the same notes that were being passed in that area.

Several days later, I called Harvey and told him I was interested in purchasing between 50,000 dollars to 75,000 dollars worth of these notes. Harvey gave me a fairly good price on them and I arranged to have another meeting with him.

On the day that I met him, he told me that he was very busy, that after he closed the shop he had to buy a lot of groceries, as his wife and family were coming back from their vacation. He stated that he also had a date with a girl who expected him to take her to a night club that particular night. He stated that he also had a date to meet the printer and turn over the money from our sale. He thought that this would keep him quite busy.

After further negotiations there came a time that evening when Harvey came to my hotel room carrying a package. This package contained close to 75,000 dollars in counterfeit notes. Harvey was annoyed at the fact that I was examining and counting each note and he was impatient and wanted to get going. He told me that his girl friend was waiting in the lobby and he would have to purchase some groceries before the stores closed. About this time, agents entered our room and placed both Harvey and I under arrest. Harvey did not have a prior criminal record and certainly appeared that he was in a state of shock. Agents attempted to question him but could not get coherent answers.

About this time, I told one of the more experienced agents that Harvey had many problems and to try to solve them as quickly as possible because Harvey had a meeting with the printer and the printer might become suspicious if Harvey did not keep the appointment. The agent established rapport with Harvey and the first thing that was accomplished was to allow Harvey to go to the lobby and quickly break the date with his girl friend. Harvey then was allowed to get the groceries into his apartment before his wife came home. We also managed to let Harvey meet his wife and get her and the children home.

Harvey was previously advised of his Constitutional rights. He stated that he wanted to get the whole matter off his mind and fully cooperate. He told the agent that he had to meet a man called Everett at a downtown bar and turn over the buy money to him. He stated Everett was the printer and the plant was in Ev's basement.

Harvey was allowed to make this meeting at which time both

Figure 7. Author and prisoner at time of arrest.

Everett and Harvey were taken into custody. Everett at first denied that he knew anything about counterfeiting. He was told that a search warrant would be obtained for his home. This upset Everett quite a bit because he had just that morning finished printing several hundred thousand in counterfeit money and never bothered to clean up the press in his basement or take the plates off the press. He realized that all the necessary evidence was at his home and he decided to cooperate. He stated that before he gave any information, he wanted to know if there was an agent Motto still in the Secret Service. When asked why, he stated that he knew Motto as a State Police officer in New York State at a time when he was a county police officer and further that they had renewed their acquaintance when he and Motto both joined the Marine Corps. It was not made known to him immediately that I was the one doing the undercover work but he was told that Motto was still in the Secret Service and they would bring him up at a future date.

The next day, we converged on the big mansion that Everett had owned. We found enough contraband to fill a truck. Plates, negatives and money were all over the cellar and it was understandable why Everett had to cooperate, as he had no way of disposing of the evidence left in his home. Certain information was needed from the residents of the town in connection with the case. All of the residents gave their complete cooperation with the understanding that after the trial was over, they fully intended to take care of Everett and his family. Immediately after his incarceration, Everett's wife was put on Welfare and she was paid as an instructor for the dancing lessons she gave the children of the town.

I visited with Everett at the Federal prison sometime later. We renewed old acquaintances and I asked Everett if I met him while I was working undercover, could I convince him that I was an ex-police officer gone wrong. Everett laughed and said I could never have convinced him in a million years that I was not working undercover, regardless of the circumstances under which we met.

It was not long afterward that Everett wrote of his exploits as a counterfeiter, for a national publication.

There is no doubt in my mind that this case was really made

Figure 8. State police officer examining counterfeit materials used in multi-million dollar counterfeit case. Photo lab in the cellar of home in Figure 4.

by the agent who was able to convince Harvey that he should cooperate with the Government. He apparently handled Harvey properly and was able to gain his confidence. Harvey was not a pushover in any sense. He was a big man who had been around quite a bit, even though he did not have a criminal record. Had he been handled improperly in the beginning, he certainly would not have brought the agents to the meeting with Everett. Up to that time, we did not have any evidence to indicate that Ev was a counterfeiter.

Figure 9. Printing press used by counterfeitor being removed from plant.

Chapter 3

THE UNDERCOVER AGENT
FALLACIES

It is becoming more necessary today to solve cases by using undercover agents (roping agents) than ever before. Many police officers and agents feel that they do not have the proper appearance or temperment to do undercover work and avoid it as much as possible. There are a lot of fallacies connected with undercover agents. A common fallacy is that an undercover agent must be a good actor, this is not so. Acting is really not a part of undercover work. As in any other business, there is a goal and the officer must use all the means at his disposal to attain that goal. In undercover work the goal is to penetrate a certain group in order to locate the contraband. Most undercover agents do not have to change their personality or looks to accomplish what they set out to do. Another fallacy is that the undercover agent must look like a gangster. Actually, there is no such thing as "looking like a gangster." If one went through the mug files of the police departments they would find prisoners that cover just about every category. Hollywood may have a prototype of a gangster, but in reality there is no typical gangster looks. Some believe that an undercover agent must be small because all police are tall. This is another fallacy. Again, a look at the mug files will show that there are as many tall people arrested as there are short ones. Certainly, size does not make a gangster or a policeman. Another fallacy is that an undercover agent must be a big spender in order to be successful in his operation. This is not true because sometimes people will become just as suspicious of a big spender as they will with one who does not spend. Again, from reading over police files and from experience with defendants, we learn that there are many defendants who are quite tight with their money, even though it comes easy to them and in making purchases they drive just as hard a bargain as a man who is on a legitimate salary. There is another fallacy that an undercover agent must be uneducated because all gangsters have very little education. This, of course, is ridiculous. I can recall the old nursery rhyme and fit it in quite well with arrests I have made. I recall arresting poor men, rich men, begger men and thieves. A number of lawyers, doctors and Indians (not necessarily chiefs). Probably, the only category I cannot account for is the candlestick maker, which appears to be a dying art, but certainly every other type of employment has been well represented in past arrests.

FITTING THE MAN TO THE JOB

Practically any agent or police officer can do undercover work providing he is fitted into the proper case and he is given the necessary cover. This does not necessarily mean that every police officer can work every case. It requires a supervisor knowing the ability of the officer or agent that he is about to assign and a genuine knowledge of the suspect and locale of where the case may take place.

Most officers would welcome the opportunity to do undercover work. Sometimes they are never given this opportunity because someone has tagged them as an average police officer. A man should be given the opportunity to do undercover work by starting on a small case. It will really be surprising to see how many so-called "average cops" can be successful in working undercover.

Harris worked with me for several years. He was an extremely intelligent agent and looked like the college type or successful businessman type. I was continually looking for a case to give him undercover experience because he was a supervisor and he certainly wanted to work as many undercover cases as possible. He knew before long he would have to break in the newer agents and there was no substitute for actual undercover experience.

One day, a prominent public relations man came to my office to give some counterfeiting information. He shall remain anonymous (he probably will never forgive me for not revealing his identity). We will call him Marty. Marty stated that in the course of his business he had met a prominent Latin who was a refugee in this country. This man, whom shall be known as Don Carlo, had a plan to counterfeit the currency of his mother country and to flood the country with these counterfeits. He felt this plan would ruin the economy of his country and thereby cause the ouster of the dictator who had been in power for a number of years. His plan was received with enthusiasm by quite a few Americans and they were happy to be of help to him. One man made a beautiful set of negatives for the currency and from these negatives a set of plates were made. Don Carlo was looking for a printer who would print the currency for him. He apparently obtained enough money from his sentimental backers to finance this counterfeiting venture. The one fact that all these people did not know was that the Secret Service is charged with the suppression of not only American currency but foreign currency as well. Marty was aware of this and not only gave us the information but was willing to introduce an agent to Don Carlo. The agent would pose as the owner of a printing plant who would print the currency from the plates supplied by Don Carlo.

This was the ideal time to use Harris on an assignment. He certainly did not have to look like anything but a plain businessman who was willing to do something in the gray area to make an extra dollar. One of my ex-counterfeiters allowed me to use his printing plant to be shown to Don Carlo in the event he wanted to see it.

The introduction went off splendidly. There were several meetings in New York and in Washington, D. C., where Don Carlo lived. This was the type of case that would not arouse any indignations because it appeared that Don Carlo's motives were patriotic. Fortunately, on one of the meetings, Don Carlo confided to Harris that when the printing was finished he planned to sell many of the counterfeits and make sure that his future was taken care of.

Don Carlo delivered the negatives and plates to Harris and Don Carlo was not shown as the patriot he pretended to be, but as just another counterfeiter. Don Carlo and the people who helped him were convicted and duly sentenced. Marty was quite happy with himself for the favor he did for us. He approached me one day and we talked about a reward. Marty said that he was expecting a reward. I asked him what he wanted. He replied that he wanted a

United States Treasury check in the amount of $202.12, no more or no less. This request had me stymied. I knew he was a good public relations man and that his stock and trade was publicity. He confided that the Internal Revenue Service of the Treasury Department was requesting $202.12 which they said he owed them. He thought it would be wonderful if he could get the Secret Service, which is also a part of the Treasury Department, to issue him a check in that amount. He in turn would present the check to the Internal Revenue. He explained that it was poetic justice.

I knew if this check was issued, Marty would have a press conference and the whole matter would become a three-ring circus. Marty was good natured about the refusal. I did manage to get him $212.12 in cash. He made sure he brought a few friends to the office when he was paid, this seemed to take care of the matter very well. Harris made many more cases thereafter and was a living example that there are no prototypes for undercover agents.

OBTAINING COVER

One of the big problems in working an undercover case is obtaining the necessary cover. Very few police organizations have the funds to rent homes, stores or set up business houses for the purpose of obtaining the necessary cover for the agent working the case. Obtaining this cover is everyone's job in the department. This is accomplished by police officers and agents making friends in various types of businesses and trades.

Shortly after World War II, I had been assigned to work undercover in various cities in the United States. There was not too much trouble in meeting suspects. The big problems was to find a place to consummate the deal. Hotel rooms had been used to a point where it was no longer safe to suggest them. Most suspects were afraid to go into a private dwelling for fear that police officers could be around and not be seen.

After working for years in straight investigations, an agent or police officer calls on a lot of business houses. Here is where he can make friends and get permission to use some of their space for an undercover assignment. I had made many friends in the check cashing business. These were stores set up throughout the city for the purpose of cashing all types of checks for a fee. Out of necessity they carry large sums of money on the premises and naturally are duly protected by bulletproof glass, cages and steel doors. The friends I had made in this business were very happy to receive telephone calls for me and would also allow me behind the counter to pose as an employee. Whenever I made a deal out of town in an undercover capacity, I would always suggest that I could handle larger "lots" if the contraband was brought to New York. I would give the phone number and address of one of the check cashing agencies as a place where I could be reached. I would explain that the agency was actually "a bookie joint" and that cashing checks was just a "front." Very often, the people from out of town would come in to look at the premises and they were generally convinced that this would be a good place to consummate a sale because the money was readily available. This is merely one type of business an officer could use. I am sure in various cities throughout the country, there are enough good citizens who would allow their premises to be used for police officers to receive telephone calls, messages and in some cases, to consummate a deal. This has to be engineered by the man on the street. It is everyones responsibility to develop the necessary cover for a roping case. The responsibility will generally fall on the "street man" who is in touch with responsible business people on a daily basis.

A large counterfeiting deal was set up by an undercover agent with a group from the mid-west. After several successful purchases, it was necessary to attempt to move the deal to New York because of the difficulty in working in the suspects' home town. The suspects were a group who had worked all over the country committing burglaries, robberies and peddling just about every type of contraband. They were "street smart" and very suspicious. It was necessary to come up with a novel idea in order to lure them to New York.

About that time, I had made a friend who had a large boat yard on Long Island. His business was quite large and he had many boats in adjoining lots next to his place of business. I approached him and he readily agreed to allow us to use his premises to work the deal. A cover story was sent out to the mid-west stating that the ultimate purchaser of the counterfeit notes was to be a man who had access to a lot of boats and that he had intended to take the counterfeit money, under the cover of darkness, out to a ship in the harbor which was bound for Europe.

The leader of the group asked for the telephone number of the boat yard and he secretly checked it out, he then came to New York and looked over the premises. Not satisfied with what he saw, he had two or three of his group also come out and look the place over. Of course, while he looked at it, there was a lot of legitimate business going on and the suspects agreed that this would be a good place to consummate the deal. From our point of view, it was an excellent location due to the fact that on the appointed day, agents and police officers were dressed in work overalls and positioned on various boats in and around the yard. The contraband was brought into the area. A deal was consummated right outside the boat yard. It was very easy to effect the arrests. One of the suspects had a loaded .45 automatic which was cocked and ready to fire but he never had the opportunity to use it because the yard was saturated with police officers. The arrests were made quickly and without incident.

UNDERCOVER TELEPHONES

Receiving telephone calls from suspects is an important part of any undercover case. A suspect legitimately wants a number from the undercover agent so he can contact him when and if the contraband arrives. Police officers and agents involved in undercover work should use every effort and means at their disposal to find places where they can receive messages. Undercover telephones are recommended in various offices. However, there are certain drawbacks to these telephones, if they are not used properly. They normally have to be in a place where someone will answer them. It has to be a telephone that cannot be checked and must be available on a twenty-four hour basis. The person answering the telephone must be knowledgeable and be aware of what calls might come in so that the telephone can be answered properly.

Figure 10. A. E. Whitaker (left) and author examine seizure of counterfeit notes.

AGENT'S ATTITUDE

The undercover agent must approach his assignment with the idea that he is buying and the suspect is selling and he should act accordingly. In the average sale, whether it is contraband or a legitimate item, there are very few people who are willing to put up money in advance, especially if it involves large sums of money. In most cases, the suspect will always ask the undercover agent to "front" the money. The stock answer for an undercover agent is that he has no assurance that he will, in fact, get a delivery and further it is very possible that someone will try to steal his money. He also explains that the money is not his and that he has no recourse to the law in the event someone decides to trick him. Most suspects will understand this because they themselves will rarely put up money in advance to purchase the contraband that they are selling.

Undercover agents must learn that they do not do everything that the suspect asks them to do. Very often, new agents or police officers working undercover want to be agreeable in order to make the case. Sometimes, this has the reverse effect. Suspects will become suspicious of a buyer who will meet them at any hour of the day or night under any circumstances and pay for the item in advance. Most people purchasing contraband drive hard bargains and are as careful about the sale as they would be in purchasing legitimate items. Many undercover agents have lost cases simply because they agreed with the suspect on many things that were not normal, thereby making the suspect suspicious. When a suspect becomes suspicious he will try various means to "check out" the prospective purchaser. If he does not receive the right answers, he will either try to steal his money or drop him completely.

MEETINGS WITH SUSPECTS

Most suspects have one thing in mind and that is to dispose of the contraband that they possess, at the best price possible. They generally do not want to socialize with the prospective buyer and are not interested in having the buyer meet too many people in their particular group. Although they are anxious to dispose of the contraband, they do not want any prospective purchaser to know too much about their operation. Other than handling the specific sale, they are usually fairly "close-mouthed."

Frequent meetings are desirable between the suspect and the undercover agent. However, in average cases, these meetings should not be too long and the agent should not be put on display where there is a possibility of someone recognizing him. In other words, it is not necessary for the agent to live with the suspect. He should keep in mind that he is a customer buying an item and after there is a "meeting of the minds," the sale should be consummated.

ADVANCE MONEY

There are occasions when it becomes absolutely necessary for an agent to advance some of the money. These are special cases that cannot be worked any other way. It is usually because the suspect has been the victim of an undercover agent on a previous occasion and he feels that most government agencies will not "front the money" under any circumstances. Each case must be judged on its own merits. Usually, the supervisor makes this decision. He takes into account how much genuine money is available to him and what results he expects from the case. If he has an opportunity to apprehend a major violator, he may find out that it is worthwhile to gamble with advance money.

DISGUISES AND PROPS

It is not necessary for the agent to wear disguises, invent tall stories or make use of elaborate settings. The undercover agent can question the informant about what he can expect from the suspect. The informant would know if the agent needed a special type car, special clothing or anything extra to make the case.

Unfortunately, most Federal and City police departments do not have a wardrobe department or prop room. Here again, the undercover agent must use his imagination to acquire the necessary props. Very often prisoners are arrested and much of their personal effects are left in the file folder, such as cards, memberships in lodges, union books, etc. Periodically, they are thrown away when the prisoner indicates he has no further need for them. These book and cards can be altered to fit the undercover agent and he can use them as identification if necessary. Many motor vehicle bureaus will give licenses to various agents and police officers in fictitious names in order to further an investigation. Some agents find a simple pair of horn rimmed glasses, mustache or sideburns give them the necessary appearance needed in a particular case.

Information had been received at a local Secret Service office that counterfeit notes were being distributed by a man who owned a barber shop in a small town in Pennsylvania. The Service was not successful in finding an informant who would make an introduction for an agent to meet the barber. The Service decided to send an agent into the town to see if he could become acquainted with the barber. He stayed in town several days and was unsuccessful in finding anyone in the small town who would introduce him to the barber. Finally, he decided he needed a haircut and went into the barber shop to get it. He was immediately spotted as a stranger and everyone in the barber shop was suspicious of him. He indicated to the barber that he was from out of town and that he was wanted by the police and had to "lay low" for several weeks. This apparently did not impress the barber too much. After finishing with the haircut, he allowed his wallet to fall back into the seat of the barber chair. Before leaving the wallet, he had loaded it with slips indicating that he owed money to various people, lottery tickets and a letter from an out-of-town parole board advising him to report on a certain date. He left the barber shop and returned several hours later. At this time he was cordially greeted by the barber who had found his wallet and looked through it. The barber returned the wallet and invited him in the back room to talk business.

Within a week, the agent was successful in making a substantial purchase of counterfeit money. The barber and his associates were arrested and there was no problem about the protection of an informant in this case.

The props used by the agent were not elaborate. However, they were very effective in convincing the barber that he was not a legitimate person and would be the type of person who would be interested in purchasing contraband.

AUTOS AND RENTED CARS

In connection with undercover work it becomes necessary to supply the undercover agent with an automobile. Very often, this automobile stays with the agent for a considerable amount of time and it is surprising how quickly the information on the automobile is spread throughout the underworld. Many people connected with the syndicate have ways of checking out a license number or a telephone number and it is important for the undercover car to be registered in a fictitious name, keeping in mind that suspects will attempt to check it out.

It has been noted in the past few years that the suspects are renting automobiles or using stolen cars to carry on their work. They are very wary about using their own car, as a license check will immediately identify them. In many cases, especially involving counterfeit money or narcotics, the car is subject to seizure. The suspects know this and would rather not jeopardize their own automobile, hence the increase in hiring or leasing cars by underworld characters. Police departments should also give some thought to leasing cars in fictitious names when doing undercover work. Before working an undercover case with an automobile, the undercover agent should have a member of his department search the car thoroughly. It is surprising how many little things could be left in an automobile which could arouse the suspicion of a suspect who rides in the car. The undercover agent driving the car on a day-to-day basis often overlooks little things such as official forms, identification cards for parking, office envelopes, etc. Any of these articles could fall under the seat of the car and be found by a suspect, if he is suspicious.

TESTIMONY AT TRIAL

Undercover agents have a tremendous responsibility in police work. Generally, it is their testimony that convicts the violator.

All police officers must tell the truth when called upon in a court of law. Truth is also stressed with an undercover agent. It is generally his testimony dealing with the day-by-day meetings and conversations he has with suspects that will influence a jury into a conviction. Any deviation from the truth at any time during the case or trial is unconscionable on the part of the agent. Agents are sometimes tempted to say something that is not true in order to possibly hide the identity of the informant. This may be a white lie in his estimation but it is perjury under the law and certainly should be avoided. Informants sometimes think that their identity can be kept secret by the undercover agent inventing lies while testifying in court. It should be explained to the informant that no one, especially a police officer has a license to lie in court. If it is that important to hide the identity of the informant, it is far better to lose the case than to reveal the informant's identity. You will note that the jury will intently listen to every word given in testimony by an undercover agent. They realize this witness is risking his life every time he works undercover. They are inclined to believe everything he says. The agent must realize that he has a tremendous responsibility not to deviate one iota from the truth.

INSTRUCTIONS TO AGENT

Supervisors who send agents out to do undercover work should give them a specific target and specific instructions as to what is expected of them. The instructions should not be too complicated and should be easily understood. The undercover agent should be given a certain amount of latitude and should be encouraged to use as much judgment as is necessary in keeping with the original instructions.

Probably the most important time in the whole undercover case is the first five seconds when the suspect is introduced to the agent. It is in these first few seconds that the suspect makes a "snap judgment" and decides whether or not he wants to do business with this person. The agent in most cases should be friendly and affable but should not overdo it. The suspect takes many things into consideration during his first meeting with the undercover agent. He knows he has very little time to decide whether or not this person would be someone he could sell contraband to. He takes into consideration the man's looks, the way he talks, the way he acts, the type of introduction he received and the availability of the contraband. If after reviewing these things, he decides he wants to do business with this new acquaintance, he will enter into a conversation with him. The agent generally cannot sell himself to the suspect if the suspect is suspicious. Some agents occassionally arouse suspicion by saying the wrong thing at the wrong time.

OVERSELLING THE AGENT

There are times when informants oversell the agent to the suspect with expressions such as, "he is one of the best safe crackers in the country" or "he is an expert on explosives." Introductions such as these can put the agent in a difficult position. Very often, the suspect will want the agent to accompany him on some illegal enterprise. Agents should have answers for situations such as these in advance. In the event they come up, agents can then make excuses and still keep contact and good relations with the suspect. Sometimes agents can get involved in compromising positions if they are not careful.

I had been trying to make a purchase of counterfeit money for several months from a mid-town character in New York called Spats. Spats lived in a cheap hotel, handled all kinds of contraband and was a well-known pimp in the neighborhood.

On this particular day, I pulled up in front of Spats' hotel. He was standing by the entrance. He approached me and asked me what I was doing and I said nothing in particular. He said, wait a minute, I have something for you. I was under the impression that this would be the counterfeit money I had sought from him for some time. Instead, he came out of the hotel several minutes later with two obvious prostitutes and asked them to get into my car. I asked him where we were going. He said, "to Pittsburgh," and I said, "to get the counterfeit money?" He said, "no, just to spend a few days with these girls out of town." Spats had already thrown his own suitcase in my car and was ready to leave. I told Spats that I had not planned on going away for a couple of days and it would be necessary for me to contact my boss before I went. Spats was under the impression that I worked for a lottery bank.

I went to the hotel lobby, faked a telephone call and came out all excited. I told Spats that it was a good thing that I had made the telephone call because my boss had been arrested. I had to go immediately to the courthouse and arrange for bail. I told Spats that I would call him just as soon as I could get free. Spats and the girls got out of the car and stated they would wait for my telephone call.

It was very easy, several hours later, to call and cancel the trip because of problems that had arisen in connection with the arrest.

In order to show the problems in some undercover cases, it might be beneficial to carry the Spats case a little further.

There came a time when Spats told me the counterfeit money was available and we could go pick up the notes. He did not tell me where we were going but just directed me while I was driving. We found ourselves entering a main thoroughfare in Bronx, New York. This had me worried because I had worked in that neighborhood several weeks before. I made a case from three principal distributors who were at this time out on bail. Sure enough, Spats directed me to a liquor store where the three defendants made their headquarters. He asked me to stop the car in front of the store. I did not stop but kept on going for several blocks and then turned out of the neighborhood. All this time Spats was screaming. After I stopped the car, I shouted at Spats and told him that I was familiar with the people in the liquor store, that I had owed them several thousand dollars. I claimed if I ever made an appearance there, I would be killed. Spats stated that he understood and he would go and get the money and bring it to me and not say anything about my presence in the neighborhood.

A short time later, Spats came back, gave me the counterfeit money that I had ordered and asked me where I was going. I stated I was going downtown and he asked me to do him a favor. He had a package of counterfeit money that he wanted to give to some friends of his in a bar next to the hotel where he lived. He asked me to give one package to the waiter, one to the bartender and one to the manager. I told him I would (there appeared to be no way out of it).

I left Spats and opened up each package and put a mark on each bill so I could identify them at a later time. I proceeded to the bar and gave the packages to the people as I was directed. I never mentioned the contents as they were apparently expecting these packages.

Later a larger purchase was made from Spats and it was decided to arrest all the people involved including the waiter, the manager and the bartender. There were quite a few defendants in the case. Some pleaded guilty and some decided to go to trial.

I, as the undercover agent, was the principal witness. I told the story of getting the counterfeit money from Spats and distributing the money to the people in the bar. After the Government's case was finished, the judge directed an acquittal of the bartender, the waiter and the manager. All the other defendants were convicted. The judge, after the trial, called me into his chambers and explained that there was no doubt in his mind as to the guilt of the people he acquitted but stated that there was nothing in my testimony that indicated that these people knew they were, in fact, receiving counterfeit money. He felt certain that the jury would convict them and in the absence of any conversation about counterfeit money, he felt they should be given the benefit of the doubt.

Situations similar to the above have come up several times since then. The action of the judge taught me a good lesson. In subsequent cases, I made certain that the people who were getting the notes knew that they were counterfeit. In some cases, we looked at the notes, examined them and discussed why we thought they were particularly good or bad counterfeits.

PROPER DRESS BY THE AGENT

Agents working undercover should be very careful of the way they dress. Undercover agents can check with the informant and learn how the suspect and his associates dress. It would be well not to overdress or to be too conservative. There are some cases that necessitate agents wearing sandals, sweaters, beards, etc. There are other cases where the suspects all wear business suits, collar and tie, etc.

NEGOTIATING WITH SUSPECT

Agents should keep in mind the entrapment angle in the opening conversation with the suspect. They should never indicate to the suspect that they are seeking counterfeit notes or other contraband. It is presumed that this conversation has already occurred between the informant and the suspect which would preclude the agent from asking for a specific item. Generally, the suspect will ask the agent if he has seen the sample and if he is satisfied with it. The conversation then will generally drift to a price. The agent at this time can indicate that for various reasons he was not satisfied with the sample and request that he be supplied with additional samples. He can indicate that he was not satisfied with the original sample for various reasons. The samples that we are talking about could be in the form of counterfeit notes, narcotics, alcohol or any other item of contraband.

After the sample is shown, the agent should ask about the price. The price normally fluctuates according to the amount of contraband that is being purchased. In the case of conterfeit notes, a price of twenty-five dollars is fair when purchasing one thousand dollars or less. As the amount increases, the price should decrease. In purchasing counterfeit notes, the price could drop as much as ten dollars per hundred when purchasing in lots of twenty-five thousand dollars or fifty thousand dollars. If the suspect gives a good price, it is not necessary to argue the price. In other words, the agent should "play it on the level." If it is too high, he should say so and if the price is right, he should indicate that he is satisfied.

In negotiating for the purchase of contraband, the undercover agent should not appear to be the "big man." One of the principal reasons is that the "big man" should be in a position to make a major decision. If this decision cannot be made, the agent would have to give an excuse. It would be far better for the agent to indicate that there are other people involved and that he is just a middleman working on a commission. If during the negotiations, the situation calls for a decision about advance money or place of delivery, the agent can always say he will check with "his people" to see if they are satisfied. This would be a major decision and one which would normally require approval from someone else who is supplying the money. The suspect always tries to make things convenient for himself.

As to the method and place of delivery, the agent can agree to almost anything with the provision that he has to check with "his people." If the arrangements are not suitable to the agency conducting the investigation, the agent working undercover can go back to the suspect and say that "his people" are not satisfied. If the suspect is adamant, the agent can agree with him and still keep negotiations open for another time, stating that he will look for different backers because the people he has been working for are impossible. When the door is left open in this manner, the agent can contact the suspect at any time with a new proposition.

Unless there is a specific case that warrants an agent acting as "Mr. Big," the average undercover case calls for the agent playing down his importance. This sometimes has a reverse effect. The suspect may believe that the agent really is big and important and that he is purposely trying to conceal his own importance.

A group of counterfeit note distributors were anxious to dispose of 250,000 dollars in counterfeit twenties. Two of their group had been arrested and money was needed for bail, lawyers and other incidentals. They were very anxious to make a deal but at the same time they were extremely careful. They certainly did not need another arrest.

An informant had introduced me to one of the group and I immediately started to negotiate for the purchase of the counterfeits that they had. I was quoted a price of eight dollars per hundred which was a fairly good price. I was told to get my money ready and to be on a designated street corner at a certain hour. I would then be picked up by a member of the group and driven to an unknown location where, in some manner, the money would be delivered to me. The whole idea was preposterous. However, I did not know if I was being tested. I mentioned that everything sounded all right to me and I would give my answer the following day.

The next day, I met four of the group and at this time I told them that the people who were putting up the money would have no part of the suggested arrangements. The group became annoyed when they learned that I was just a commission man acting for someone else. They tried hard to persuade me to do business their way. I confessed that I could see nothing wrong with their setup. I said I knew I could trust the group and felt that they would keep their word.

I met with them on succeeding nights and carried the story that my people were too suspicious and would not do business. I mentioned that I would try to find another buyer for the notes.

In the weeks that followed, I made it a point to strengthen my relationships with the group and I was always pleased to hear that they still had the counterfeits. When it became apparent that they needed money in a hurry for an impending trial, I told them about the Texan I had just met. He had made a good score on some stolen securities in New York City and was anxious to bring some counterfeits back home. The group was so pleased about this prospect that they were willing to drop the price to seven dollars per hundred. I told them the only problem was that the Texan was leaving the following morning and it would be necessary to make a fast deal at the airport. This did not set too well with the group and they decided to have a conference. After an hour they had made a decision. Ed, the spokesman for the group, told me they had decided to sell the counterfeits to the Texan. They had one condition and that was that I would have to make the delivery. For my trouble, I was to receive one dollar per hundred. It was agreed that I would meet the Texan at the airport. I was to assure myself he had the "buy" money. Ed would arrive at the airport and put the counterfeits in a locker. He would turn the key over to me. The Texan would go with me to the box, pick up the notes and pay me for them immediately. I would meet Ed and give him the genuine money. When Ed told me of the plans, I could hardly keep a straight face, I could not have made better plans myself. In their attempt to make a foolproof sale, they had boxed themselves in nicely.

The next day, all that was needed was an undercover agent with a ten gallon hat and a pair of boots. Ed, true to his promise, arrived on time, deposited a package in the locker box and gave me the key. He was accompanied by two more of the group and none of them wanted to meet the Texan. The arrests went off smoothly. All of the group eventually made bail, but needed money more than ever. They switched from counterfeiting to armed robbery. Before the counterfeit case came to trial, one was killed during an attempted holdup. His partner was arrested and received ten to fifteen years. Two others were convicted of burglary and received long prison terms. They eventually pleaded guilty to the counterfeit charges. They were convinced that the Texan was a Texas Ranger on an undercover assignment.

Not being the "big man" paid off in this case. Again, it gave me the opportunity to turn down their original proposal but still stay in their good graces.

Officers working undercover should be alert at all times, with particular references to license numbers of cars that appear in the area, faces of people that they meet, names, addresses and telephone numbers. Sometimes covering agents cannot get this information because of the distance they maintain from the action. When it is practical, the undercover officer should make notes as soon as possible. If he is in a public place it would be very easy for him to excuse himself, go to the men's room and jot down a telephone number or license number. When he leaves the scene of the action, he should immediately go to a typewriter and make as many notes as he can remember to aid him in making his report.

CROSS-EXAMINATION AT TRIAL

In a court case, it is very hard for the defense attorney to find something to "hang his hat on" when he is cross-examining an undercover agent. He, therefore, must rely on such things as what time was it, how far away was the man from you, how was he dressed and other seemingly insignificant items. He has to do this because he generally cannot weaken the main portion of the agent's testimony. After he asks the small details of the under-cover agent, he will question the covering agents along the same line to try to show discrepancies in times, distances, etc.

ADVANTAGE IN OBTAINING SAMPLES

In attempting to make an undercover case, the officer working undercover usually tries to obtain a sample of the contraband that is being sold. This is natural because much of the contraband comes in different grades. Narcotics sometimes is pure and other times it has been cut to a point where it has little or no effect on the user. Counterfeit money runs from very good to very poor. Therefore it is necessary for the undercover agent to see what he is buying before he can offer a price for the merchandise. If the agent can acquire enough samples or a small purchase, his case is made. On the second or third buy he can be a little harder to get along with and in the event any changes are made by the seller, the agent can demand that the sale be handled in the same manner as the first one. At the time of the second buy, the agent can complain about shortages on the first buy and the quality of the merchandise. This would put the seller on the defensive. The agent then could demand to examine the contents of the next buy more closely and could demand enough time to make a closer count. If the buy is large enough, for example in the purchase of counterfeit money a buy of 100,000 dollars was ordered, this would be large enough to warrant delivery by more than one person. Generally, the principal distributors would want to accompany the seller to protect their own interests.

Regardless of what arrangements have been made in advance, the suspect will continually try to get advance money from the agent. In very rare cases it will be necessary for the agent to "front" his money. The argument that the money is not his and that he has no recourse if the delivery is not made is a valid argument in spite of the fact it is being used all the time. The suspects will try to get a portion of the money in advance. Again, this should not be done, using the same argument. Suspects will sometimes try to have a mutual acquaintance, possibly the informant, as the person who will hold the money until the deal is consummated. This situation should be talked over with the informant before the transaction is effected. If at all possible, the informant should be kept away from the scene at the time of the buy. This should satisfy both the undercover agent and the informant. If the informant is not at the scene, this may help him with his explanation of why the deal culminated in an arrest. It is also a good idea for the informant not to be present because at the time of the delivery, if the suspect is the least bit suspicious, he may wish to have the informant make the delivery to the agent. If the delivery is made by the informant, it is necessary for the informant to testify at the trial in order to maintain the chain of evidence. If the informant does not wish to be exposed, all efforts should be made to keep him away from the scene of the buy, especially if an arrest is anticipated.

SIGNALS AND CONTROLLING PLACE OF DELIVERY

The undercover agent should try to control the place of delivery. This is a very important part of the case. Deliveries in private clubs, in suspects' homes, in cellars and similar places provide an impossible situation. In order to make a case successful, it is necessary that the buy be covered so the covering agents know when to make the arrest. Public places are very desirable, such as bus stops, railroad stations, airports, restaurants, busy stores, etc. A hotel room is ideal, providing the agent can pick the hotel and the room and further can arrange for agents to be in adjoining rooms. The suspect will try to make a delivery at a time and place that is convenient for him. The agent can use the argument that he is skeptical of a private home or private club because he is afraid of being robbed. If the suspect insists that the agent accompany him to a secluded spot, the agent can then tell the suspect that he will go with him but will not bring his money. In this way, it will be necessary for the suspect to accompany the agent back to where the agent's money is and, of course, this spot can be covered by other agents who can make the arrest after the necessary signal is given. Signals have always been a "pet peeve" with me. It was always something I took for granted. We have been using signals for years and it was something that was casually mentioned before going out on the case. I had one experience that made me give more thought to signals and in the ensuing years I have seen where the misinterpretation of a signal can cause havoc with a case.

Tom was a lovable character, he spent most of his time around the race tracks when the racing season was on. He was not a tout or bookmaker but he enjoyed the "Sport of Kings" and found that he could watch the races, bet and also carry on his "receiving" business at the track. Tom can best be described as a typical Damon Runyon character.

In connection with an investigation I was conducting far away from New York City, I had run into Tom. He immediately recognized I was a New Yorker and accused me of "talking funny." The business I had with Tom was not very important. He allegedly attended a crap game in which counterfeit money had been passed. I had contacted everyone I heard that was connected with the game and I did not get anywhere with the investigation. If Tom gave me any useful information, it would have helped because there was very little else to go by. After our official conversation, Tom and I had a sandwich together and had a friendly chat. I never saw or heard from him until five years later.

Tom came into the office and was trying to find out if I was still employed there. He did not know my name but was trying to describe me to the clerk when I walked in. We renewed our acquaintance and Tom and I left the office for a cup of coffee. Tom told me that he appreciated the fact that I did not cause him any trouble after our first encounter and felt that he owed me a favor.

He stated that an acquaintance of his was in a position to get counterfeit money. His friend who we will call Dan was quite a well-known comic on the Broadway scene and was heavily indebted to the shylocks. His friend, Dan, had been offered a "dealership" in handling counterfeit money and was looking for customers. I asked Tom to introduce me to Dan. Tom refused stating that he would be in trouble if it ever developed I was an agent and Dan was arrested as a result of doing business with me. Tom stated that Dan would be an "easy mark" because this was his first venture into crime. We had a long discussion about the possibility of an introduction. I could see that Tom could not introduce me and I asked Tom to keep me advised of Dan's activities.

About this time, I had received a visit from another man, Patsy M., who wanted to do me a favor. He was from out of town. In his day, he was a well-known racketeer on the West coast. He was not doing too well financially, he was getting old and found it very difficult to "make ends meet" in New York. I asked him if he wanted to settle up with me before he left. He said he would do anything within reason but it would have to be done quickly because he intended to return to the West coast.

I called Tom and asked if he would introduce Patsy to Dan. Tom said he had no objection if Patsy was not a Federal agent. Patsy was flattered when he heard this, and agreed to meet Dan.

Tom eventually introduced Patsy to Dan and before long they became fairly good friends. Just before Patsy was scheduled to leave for the West coast, we arranged a chance meeting on Broadway. Patsy introduced me to Dan as an old friend who served time with him in a federal penitentiary. I caught Dan's act in several night clubs and managed to have a drink with him on a few occasions. Off stage, Dan was the saddest comic I have ever seen, for a man who was paid to make people laugh he looked like the personification of Digger O'dell the comic undertaker. One day he was "down in the dumps" and told me that the shylocks were pressuring him for money he owed. He was what is known on Broadway as a degenerate horse player. Every dime he earned was given to the bookmakers and shylocks. He confided in me that he had not been out of debt in the past twenty years in spite of the fact that he was working regularly and making good money. He was particularly distressed this night and asked me to accompany him to a local bar. When we got there, he showed me a ten and a twenty dollar counterfeit bill and asked me if I could use any. He said that he had a connection and could get the counterfeits in any amounts. He quoted a fairly good price and bragged that he handled hundreds of thousands of these particular notes. I knew that the note had a fairly good distribution but nowhere near what Dan had bragged about. I told him that I was interested. He then put on a very somber face and warned me that I would be killed if anything went wrong or if I "squealed." I could not keep from laughing as Dan gave a fairly amusing performance at being a tough guy. Dan took my order for 100,000 dollars in counterfeits and arranged for me to meet his friend, Whitey, who was to make the delivery.

Whitey tried to acquire the "buy money" in advance and after much haggling he agreed to deliver the notes the following day at a local hotel. We managed to get adjoining rooms for the covering agent at this hotel and we set everything up for the arrest after the delivery. Before leaving the office, the senior agent asked me what signal I would use to show that I had actually received the money. I said I would look at the package and say this "goddamn crap is no good." At the appointed time, Whitey came to my room carrying a package. I opened it and found that it contained a sizeable amount of counterfeit money. In a voice louder than normal, I said, "this junk is no good." Nothing happened, I suddenly realized that I had completely forgotten the signal. I tried everything, counting the notes out loud, complaining about the quality and trying to reduce the price. All this was causing Whitey much concern, he wanted his money and wanted to get going. In the hallway by the elevator two people were waiting for Whitey to bring them the good money. I tried stalling for five more minutes, then finally in desperation, I opened the door to the adjoining room and told the agents to come in and make the arrest. I "blew my cover sky high" and in any other case, I probably would have gotten the informant hurt or maybe killed. In this case the informant was in California and did not care whether anyone knew him or not. The men in the hallway were arrested and the following morning Dan was arrested. His arrest was the most pitiful thing we had seen in a long time. He was well respected in the entertainment field and most of his friends and associates thought he was financially well-off. Even though he managed to make bail, it was a long time before he could find work again. Although he did not appreciate it at the time, the arrest was a blessing in disguise.

Several years after his case was disposed of, I met him after one of his performances. We talked about the case and he told me that his arrest cancelled out all his debts to the shylocks. This apparently is the code of the underworld. Dan is now back on the circuit and I am certain he is still borrowing money from the shylocks. The case turned out very well but from that time on, I paid strict attention to the signal and realized through sad experience that it was one of the most important acts in the entire undercover case. The signal triggers off a series of events that hopefully ends with the seizure of the contraband and the arrests of the suspects. How about Patsy? Well, it later developed that Patsy and Dan had become old buddies during their brief acquaintance. Before Patsy left for the West coast, Dan sold him a small package of counterfeits. Patsy managed to get arrested after he passed the third note.

The signal is very important in any case. Many signals can be used. The important thing is that the signal be simple, that it can be observed from a great distance and that is cannot be misinterpreted. The idea of lighting a cigar or smoking a cigarette can be dangerous because the undercover agent can inadvertently light a cigarette thereby causing a premature arrest. Again, any signal should suffice as long as it can be easily understood.

If the agent states that the money is in the trunk of his car, the opening of the trunk is a signal that cannot be misinterpreted. Certainly it can be seen from a distance if the covering agents are careful to place themselves in a position where nothing will interfere with their line of vision.

When an area is selected for the delivery, it is a good idea for several agents to visit that area long in advance of the proposed buy. They will look for many things. One important thing is the necessary cover so that the agents covering the deal will not be exposed. Secondly, it is important to look over the area, perhaps there will be a City, State or Federal installation in the vicinity that could be used as an observation post. Sometimes in canvassing the area, agents will recall that they have a friend or relative in the neighborhood whose premises could be used. In a counterfeiting case, it is a good idea to canvass the business section of the neighborhood with a view of trying to locate a print shop which could be responsible for the production of the notes that are being sold. This is especially true if the neighborhood is selected by the suspect.

CRIME IN THE PRINT SHOP

At this point, it might be a good idea to discuss the different crimes that can be committed in print shops. Sometimes officers go through a whole career in a police department without ever being inside a printing establishment. Today, more than ever, the print shop is responsible for many and varied types of crimes. In order to keep an illegal lottery going in a city it is necessary to have a printer make the tickets. This applies to any type of lottery: football, baseball, basket ball, etc. Very often, the printing of lottery tickets is what leads the printer into a real life of crime. He learns that printing lottery tickets is far more profitable than printing wedding invitations or business cards. Some printers who are having financial difficulties are approached to print lottery tickets merely to see how far they will go. After the lottery tickets, they are propositioned about printing pornography in the form of pictures and books. This too, can be very profitable for the printer. It is then very easy for the syndicate or group to proposition the printer on making counterfeit checks, counterfeit bonds, counterfeit stock certificates, birth certificates, marriage certificates, credit cards, driver's licenses, bills of sale and counterfeit money. The printing of counterfeit licenses and ownership cards may look like small items but they are very important to groups who steal automobiles. After an automobile is stolen, a member of the group is supplied with counterfeit identification and driver's licenses. He is then supplied with a counterfeit bill of sale and it is very easy for the group to register the automobile in one state and then bring it over to a nearby state and reregister it again. If it becomes necessary, they are also equipped to change the serial number on the car. This same *modus operandi* can be used by the group to rent a car with false identification and then proceed to get it legitimately registerd with a counterfeit bill of sale, etc.

When a counterfeiting plant is located and the printer arrested, a complete search of the premises can be of great help to other agencies. If the arrest is made by a Federal agency, generally enough evidence is found at the plant or shop which will be of interest to State and City authorities. Complete cooperation by all agencies will help identify and break up the syndicate.

Besides looking for print shops, the neighborhood should be looked over for horse rooms, betting premises, local social clubs and the candy store or tobacco shop that has little or no stock. These are the places where the loot or contraband may be held before a delivery is made. Identifying these premises and keeping them under surveillance can be a great help at the time of the proposed buy.

ROPING BY MORE THAN ONE AGENT

For many years, various agencies have felt that one undercover case rated one undercover agent. Over the last ten or fifteen years, I have decided that if two or three people can purchase contraband from friends and acquaintances, there is no reason why two or three undercover agents cannot do the same thing without arousing any undue suspicion. Wherever possible, at least two undercover agents should be used on a case. Very often, when a single man is used, various situations can arise where he is not in a position to report it to his supervisors or to his covering agents. In a case where an undercover agent has another man along with him, he could be introduced as a partner, a chauffeur, a delivery boy or anything that will fit the particular situation. In the event the undercover agent wanted to relay information back to his headquarters, he can always make the excuse that his chauffeur has an errand to perform and the chauffeur will then be in a position to relay the necessary information to headquarters. There are times when the second or third man can be either a buyer or an expert, depending on the contraband that is being sold.

A group of counterfeiters had decided that they would print several million five cent counterfeit United States postage stamps. Like many groups before them, they were able to counterfeit the stamps. However, after the job was complete, they found it very difficult to find an outlet for their product. Most businesses and people that use large amounts of stamps use postage meters and many people who are prone to buying stamps at a discount could never use more than four or five sheets.

This particular group gave an informant a sheet of stamps to be shown as samples in the event the informant was able to interest a prospective buyer in taking over the whole lot. The informant brought the sheet of stamps to the office and it was decided to use an undercover agent to contact the group. Arrangements were made whereby the informant could introduce the suspect to the prospective buyer in a hotel in Ohio. This was the type of case where the informant could not be exposed and it was decided that the agent doing the undercover case would call in an "expert" before he actually purchased the stamps.

The meeting took place in the hotel as scheduled; the suspects were in the same hotel but in different rooms. The undercover agent was introduced to the suspect and the suspect asked the agent if he saw the samples. The agent stated that he looked at the sample sheet but before purchasing the stamps, he wanted to call in an expert to look them over before he invested his money. The suspect was a little annoyed at these arrangements. However, he checked with "his people" and it was agreed to let the expert look at the stamps.

I had posed as the expert and later that night met the suspect. He gave me the keys to his car, told me that the stamps were in the trunk and stated he would give me one hour to bring the car wherever I wished and make an examination of the stamps.

I took the car, went to the nearest Secret Service Office and discovered that there were several million counterfeit stamps in the car. I returned to the hotel and told the undercover agent in the presence of the suspect that the stamps were very poorly executed and that my advice to him was not to purchase them. The suspect became enraged at this statement and tried to convince the undercover agent that he should purchase the stamps.

He stated that he had supplied a sample well in advance of the sale and that the agent was obligated to make the purchase because his group went out of their way to bring the stamps a great distance for the sale. It was very easy for the undercover agent to explain that he went through the expense of getting an expert and that he would abide by the expert's decision. This argument went on for several hours.

The suspect on many occasions left the room to check with "his people" who were in a room nearby. When he returned each time, all offers were rejected on the grounds that the stamps were no good. After each argument, the suspect reduced the price till finally, it was down to one-fifth of the original price. The original plans were not to buy the stamps but to force the suspects to leave with the stamps and then place them under arrest while they were en route home.

The undercover agent maintained the position that the stamps were of such poor quality that buying them would not only cost him a lot of money but might also be the cause of his arrest as the expert stated the stamps would not fool anyone. During these negotiations, a telephone call was received from the informant in which he stated that the group was desperate and they had decided to come to the agent's hotel room with guns and take his money. After receiving this telephone call, the agent and I excused ourselves, left the hotel room and never returned. The suspect soon got tired of waiting for us, he joined his friends. All four of them left the hotel several hours later, got into their automobile and as soon as they attempted to leave, they were placed under arrest and the stamps which were still in the trunk were confiscated.

This is a good example of how a case can be worked with more than one agent working undercover. Certainly, in this case one man complimented the other and both their actions helped make a successful case. The defendants believed that the expert was the person who "leaked" the information to the authorities.

PREPARATION

In working undercover, everyone involved in the case should sit down for a good talk session and attempt to think of all the eventualities beforehand. In the session deliberate obstacles should be brought up in order to see how they could be handled. It is realized that every eventuality cannot be thought of beforehand. However, a discussion should be had so alternate plans could be made. There are very few cases that go according to plan. While each case seems the same on the surface, there are always last minute changes that do not become problems providing they are discussed beforehand.

An undercover agent should try as hard as possible to make the case but when it becomes apparent that the whole situation is impossible for any reason, the agent should not be afraid to walk away from the case, providing he "leaves the door open" for the suspect to contact him. No supervisor should reprimand an agent who walks away from a case. Supervisors who have worked

Figure 11. Seizure of several million counterfeit stamps. Left to right: H. Gibbs, Special Agent in Charge; A. E. Whitaker, Special Agent in Charge; and author.

undercover will understand that there are some cases that just cannot be made. Perhaps it will be necessary to try four or five times before a successful case can be made against a difficult suspect.

The counterfeit check case in the Southwest was successful because I felt that the situation in the Southwest became impossible. I first made certain that the people had a way of contacting me, then I walked away from the group. After several days of discussing it, the suspects realized they lost a good customer and then they decided to contact me to see if they could salvage the deal.

ELEMENTS OF UNDERCOVER CASES

While no two cases are exactly the same, there are certain elements that are necessary in each case. It could be boiled down to first the "introduction." This introduction is made by the informant and this is the beginning of the case. From this point on, the undercover agent is either accepted or not. In the event that he is not accepted, it might be necessary for the informant to meet the suspect at a later date without the undercover agent in order to learn why the suspect did not accept the agent at the time of the introduction. In the event the agent is not accepted, it is very easy for the informant to bring in another agent with a different cover story. This time, both the agent and informant will try to overcome any difficulties the first agent had.

After the introduction, there is a conversation about the contraband which is to be purchased. This conversation will generally result in the undercover agent seeking samples or obtaining samples. After the samples have been delivered, the undercover agent meets again with the suspect to let him know how much of a purchase he is to make. This purchase may or may not go through. This is decided before the figures are given to the suspect. If it is decided that this buy will go through, no arrests should be made and nothing should be done to arouse the suspicion of the suspect.

Usually, the first buy is a small one and the Agency does not mind losing this money in order that the undercover agent can come back on another occasion and make a larger purchase.

Generally, the second purchase is large enough to warrant not only the appearance of the suspect but also some of the people connected with him.

As previously mentioned, there comes a question of payments. Most suspects cannot handle very large buys, especially if it is necessary for them to purchase the merchandise in advance. Because the first buy proceeded smoothly, the suspect sometimes oversells the undercover agent to his connection and insists that the large buy will proceed with no trouble. Usually, the suspect will get delivery but the people who delivered the contraband to him will be in the vicinity to make certain that they receive their money after the purchase.

At the scene of the second buy when a signal is given, arrests are made, including the undercover agent and the informant, if he is present. This is a very crucial part of the entire undercover case. This is the point where the informant has to be covered up and the actions taken by the arresting agents at the scene will dictate whether or not his cover is successful. It is very important at the scene of the arrest for the arresting agents to separate the undercover agent and the informant from the rest of the group. The undercover agent usually will have been in contact with the suspect for several hours and he will undoubtedly have more information to give to the arresting agents. If he is in the company of the other prisoners, it would be very difficult for him to give this information. At the time he is separated, he should be interviewed with the informant immediately. He may be in a position to give information regarding who else is involved, where the rest of the merchandise is kept, the location of the plant, who might be waiting for the genuine money after the delivery and many other important bits of information that he has picked up during his conversation with the suspect. The above also applies to the informant who undoubtedly has been listening and talking to the suspects just prior to the delivery. If there have been any prearranged ideas on how the informant is to be covered, this is the time to put them in effect. Some suspects can be fooled and will believe almost anything that is told to them, while others who have been engaged in criminal activities for a long time will not be easily fooled. However, some effort should be made to attempt to cover the informant.

There are informants who do not object to being exposed. There can be a number of reasons why an informant feels this way. He may be leaving the area and has no intention of returning. He may feel he is as tough as any of the people he is informing on. He may have just met the suspect and does not plan to see him again. He may be a professional informant who testifies at trials and does not care what happens as long as he is paid for his services.

In cases where we are dealing with this type of informant, it is still a good idea to arrest him and the undercover agent at the scene. If after questioning, the defendants will not cooperate, the exposure of the informant and undercover agent will generally have a psychological effect on the defendants. After learning they have been doing business with an undercover agent, they may be in a position to fully cooperate. Before a situation like this can be worked out, all phases of the case must be explored to be certain that exposure will not jeopardize either the informant or the usefulness of the undercover agent.

After the arrest have been made, the prisoners, the undercover agent and the informant should be separated and, of course, the prisoners should be searched immediately on the scene for any weapons and contraband. Any vehicles that the suspects have on the scene should likewise be searched and seized, if the circumstances warrant it.

There are some cases which are accomplished very quickly, sometimes in the space of an hour or less. A quick undercover case is not unusual and sometimes fast-moving events make it important that the case is moved along as quickly as possible. This is necessary when certain information about an arrest is going to appear in a later edition of a newspaper or radio broadcast. There are occasions when the news media learns of an arrest of a violator and just before the story is published, the violator decides to cooperate, perhaps by introducing an undercover agent to another suspect. It becomes necessary to effect this introduction and sale before the next edition of the news reaches the public and announces that an arrest had been made. On the other hand, some undercover cases can last for days, weeks and even months. In the case of an undercover agent who is gathering intelligence from foreign sources or subversive information, he can be undercover perhaps for as long as several years or for as long as his identity remains secret.

There are times when an undercover agent starts on one case and stumbles onto something more important and then pursues that case even though it might not be in his own jurisdiction.

Johnny, a "top flight" narcotic agent was working in and around the Chicago area on narcotic violators. One day while still undercover, Johnny met Pete, a big hoodlum from a small town who was known to handle narcotics and other contraband.

Pete, apparently had run out of narcotics and in conversations with Johnny, propositioned Johnny on the handling of counterfeit money. Johnny felt sure the Secret Service would be interested in sending a man to work with him undercover. He took it upon himself to tell Pete that he had a friend from out East whom he was sure would make a purchase. He promised to get in touch with his friend and contact Pete as soon as his friend came to the Chicago area.

Johnny then notified his supervisor about the counterfeiting proposition and the Secret Service was notified. I was assigned to work with Johnny and a few days later we proceeded to a private club owned by Pete, outside of Chicago.

Pete showed me some sample counterfeit notes which at that time were receiving national distribution and were being passed in large quantities. We knew the source was in Chicago. We knew the suspect was a man who had been arrested many times previously for counterfeiting and was known in his own circles as Satan. All attempts to make a case against Satan at that time were futile. There was no one, that we knew, willing to effect an introduction to this man.

After the second meeting with Pete, I arranged to purchase five thousand dollars worth of counterfeit notes from him. I told him I was going back to New York and then would undoubtedly call him in a few days with a much larger order. I indicated to him that I represented a Syndicate who were anxious to make contacts in the mid-west for various kinds of contraband. Pete jumped at this opportunity to break in to what he thought was the "big time" in New York. He suggested that in the event I wanted a large amount of counterfeit notes, he would personally deliver them to New

York in company with Johnny and hoped that at that time he would be introduced to the members of the Syndicate.

About ten days later, I called Pete and told him that I needed a quarter of a million dollars worth of these counterfeits. Pete assured me that he would have no trouble obtaining the notes and asked me for a telephone number where I could be contacted. I gave him a number and the following day he called me and told me that he would be in New York the next day and he supplied me with the airline and flight number. After his original call to me, Pete was observed on two or three occasions in the company of Satan who was undoubtedly making the arrangements to get the notes to Pete for his trip to New York.

I met Pete and Johnny at the airport at the given time. Pete was impressed with the limousine that we used for this occasion and the fact that I had my own chauffeur. Pete told me that he was being very careful, that he had come armed and he had to be sure that nothing could happen to these notes because he had hocked everything he owned in order to make part payment on the notes he brought to New York, without getting payment in advance.

We proceeded to a local hotel where we made arrangements to have Pete have his own suite of rooms. While in his suite, we counted the stacks of notes and found that he had fairly close to a quarter of a million dollars. We had received several telephone calls at his room and we assured Pete that the Syndicate was getting together to pay him a visit. Although Pete was completely satisfied with all the arrangements, he was very nervous and insisted upon carrying his gun fully loaded in a shoulder holster. Just before the agents arrived to make the arrest in the hotel room, I had convinced Pete that it did not look proper for him to be wearing his gun. He surrendered his gun to me and I hid it in a closet.

The arrest was completed without incident and Pete was lodged at the Federal House of Detention in New York City. It was important that we made some sort of move before the newspapers printed the story that Pete had been arrested.

The following morning, we were able to delay his arraignment. Pete was brought to the Secret Service Office. Johnny and I both identified ourselves as Federal Agents, which was quite a shock to Pete. Pete needed time to think things out and we were pressuring him for an introduction to Satan. He assured us that nothing could be done as far as an introduction because the notes had to be paid for first and he doubted whether Satan would talk to any stranger. He admitted that Satan was the source for the counterfeit notes and agreed to cooperate, even if it was necessary to testify against Satan. In order to corroborate his testimoney, we had him make a telephone call to Satan and discuss the sale of the quarter million dollars. Satan was quite cagey over the telephone. However, enough information was recorded to convince anyone that Satan was the source of these notes.

Pete was held in very high bail and during his absence, his common-law wife ran off with another man, his private club was lost because of nonpayment of debts and all his personal belongings were stolen by another girl friend he was keeping in an apartment. All these events depressed Pete and had a tremendous psychological effect on him. He was no longer interested in making bail, he just wanted to dispose of his case as quickly as possible, serve his time and be finished with the whole mess.

As a result of the information supplied by Pete, a warrant was obtained for the arrest of Satan. Satan was arrested at his home, which was thoroughly searched. No contraband was found.

Satan knew he had been a target of the Secret Service for quite a few years. He also knew he had a close call several years before, when an excellent witness against him committed suicide. He knew a long imprisonment would separate him from his young daughter, whom he adored. All these things were running through Satan's mind when Johnny and I questioned him. In a surprisingly short time, Satan decided he would throw his lot with the government and cooperate. He said he was not responsible for the manufacturing of the counterfeit money but he could arrange to set up his source. He agreed to introduce me to his connection and he felt that he could arrange for a half million dollar delivery. The astonishing thing was he was certain he could arrange this without any "front" money. He further stated that the counterfeits would not have to be paid for until they were disposed of by me.

Satan eventually introduced me to a man whom we will call Frisco. Frisco looked like a cheap hoodlum. The conversation was completely dominated by Satan and in no time Frisco agreed to let me have a half million to take to Europe. It was agreed that I would pay for it after I returned to the States. Frisco agreed to these terms and indicated he would wait two months for the payment. We later talked this deal over at the office and all agreed that Satan was up to something. It certainly looked like the deal was all his and that Frisco was someone who took orders from him. Nevertheless, Frisco went through with his part.

About a week later, he arranged to leave a half million dollars in my car, which he had borrowed for the deal. About a month later, my brother, working in an undercover capacity, contacted Frisco and told him I was ready to dispose of the notes in France but I needed another hundred grand. The whole deal had to be consummated at once. We knew that Frisco would have to contact Satan, he did and Satan approved the deal. It was clear to us that Satan was still the boss. We confronted him with our suspicion. He vehemently denied any connection with the plant.

We then set Frisco up with another fifty thousand dollar order and placed him under arrest. He did not cooperate and after several days, made bail and was back on the street.

Satan had not been officially arraigned up to this time and he pleaded for more time and agreed to work for other agencies so he could square himself with the government. It was pointed out to him that this was "sheer madness" on his part to stay on the street without being arrested (officially) on the counterfeit charges. He still pleaded for more time and it was granted. Satan went on to make more cases for other agencies. It soon became apparent to the underworld that Satan was miraculously staying out of jail while everyone else was being arrested. Satan's double dealings came to rest one morning in a school parking lot. He was found slumped over the steering wheel of his car with six bullets in his head. The school yard was behind the same school that his daughter attended.

Frisco later went to trial and stated that he was merely a delivery boy for Satan. He stated his every action was dictated by Satan who controlled the whole counterfeiting plant. Frisco served a short term and later met a similar fate for his part in the "Satan" conspiracy.

It is refreshing to know that this whole case was made because a

Figure 12. A four-million dollar seizure of counterfeit notes.

brother agent investigating another crime saw fit to pursue information given to him by a suspect, even though it meant nothing to his Service. It is cooperation of this type from various agencies that make police work the rewarding job that it is.

We have previously discussed the fact that in most instances we felt that informants belong to the department and not to the individual officer. However this does not preclude the fact that some informants will only work with one man. This might be for a number of reasons: they are compatable, they speak the same language, the officer might have gone out of his way in the past to help this informant and so on. When an informant expresses a desire to work with a particular officer or agent, this request should be honored unless there are some strong reasons to do otherwise. If an agent and an informant have worked together successfully in the past, that is all the more reason that the informant's desire to work with this particular officer in another case be fulfilled.

I had worked in the past with an informant whom I shall call Fred. Fred was a fairly successful businessman and money is the one thing that he did not need. His business operations were always in the gray area and he had more than his share of trouble with the police. Fred, however, could not walk away from the opportunity of setting up a good deal. I had not seen Fred in some time. As a matter of fact, I was working several hundred miles from him and was promoted to a supervisor. This never stopped Fred from calling whenever he had what he thought was something I might be interested in. Knowing that Fred never exaggerated or built up a case, I always managed to find the time to see him when he called.

On this particular occasion, he called me and left word that he had some information on Treasury checks. This could have meant anything, stolen checks, forged checks or even counterfeit checks. I was not too inclined to travel a great distance to discuss the forgery of a check with him. This was a routine matter that could have been handled by anyone. Knowing full well that Fred would be peeved if I sent someone else to interview him, I made arrangements to see him the day after he called.

When we met, he explained that a day or so before, a man came into his place of business and wanted to sell him a United States Treasury check for 50 per cent of the amount shown on the check. He further stated that the man told him he was in a position to get unlimited numbers of Treasury checks and he could supply them with whatever amount the purchaser wanted. The informant stated that he did not know the man very well. However, the man was well dressed, drove a big car and looked fairly prosperous. Fred could not supply very much more information but suggested that I hang around his place of business for a few days. He felt that the suspect would come back and he would introduce me to him. I was not too inclined to spend the time there. Certain administrative duties were pressing and I felt that I should return to my office and assign a man to work with Fred. Fred would not hear of it and he insisted that I spend at least two days there as he felt that this would turn out to be something good.

In my own mind, it added up to someone who found a way to steal government checks out of the mail or was pulling some sort of swindle on the Internal Revenue and was able to obtain large refund checks. I suggested to Fred that if the suspect came into his shop, he should introduce me as a friend from New York who had a check cashing agency there and was interested in obtaining some Treasury checks. He could indicate that he discussed the proposition with me and I was interested.

On the second day, the suspect came into the store and he was introduced to me as Cal. After some general conversation, he confided that he was in a position to supply unlimited amounts of United States Treasury checks and could have them made out in any amount. He stated that they would be sent through the mail and he would see to it that they were sent to any address that I supplied to him. After Cal learned that I had my own check cashing agency, he was very anxious to do some business with me. I suggested that he and I go somewhere we could talk in private. He suggested that we go for a drive in his car. That was all right with me and we went for a two-hour drive.

I was able to learn that Cal was some kind of a United States Government employee, that he was a supervisor in some unit and that he was responsible in some way for sending out Government checks to individuals. He had found a way to arrange to have checks sent to anyone he wished. He had to use a certain name; the address could be supplied by the purchaser. The purchaser had to give Cal one-half the value of the check. Cal went on to say that it took him eighteen years to figure out how to beat the Government. He knew that his system was foolproof and that no one could get in trouble for cashing the check. I told him the whole scheme sounded incredible. However, I was willing to take a chance with one or two checks to see how they went. Cal stated that he had a check in the trunk of his car. He stopped the car, gave me keys and told me to open the trunk, that the check would be in an envelope in the trunk. Opening the trunk gave me an excellent opportunity to get his license number and find out who he was. I found the check and went back to the car. The check was made out to an Ambrose Fieler in the amount of 420 dollars. I examined the check. There was no doubt that it was genuine and it was drawn by the Veterans Administration.

A further conversation with Cal in the car revealed that Cal would let me have that particular check and after I cashed the check, I could call him and arrange to pay him. He then wanted to be supplied with a list of addresses anywhere in the country. He stated that he would arrange to send a check to each of these addresses in any amount that I wanted. His only caution was to make sure that I could get these checks out of the mail. He did not want the checks to be returned as undeliverable. I assured Cal that I could handle it and told him that I would return to New York and contact him in a day or so and supply him with the necessary list. We parted company. He again assured me that there never could be a complaint on the checks because the payees would never know that they had been issued. He gave me his home telephone number and two days later I called him and made an appointment to see him at a local hotel.

In the meantime, an exhaustive check revealed that Cal was indeed a Government employee. He was a supervisor in a unit of the Veterans Administration. His unit handled the dormant accounts of the Veterans of World War I. There were hundreds of accounts in the names of veterans who were due large sums of money. However for various reasons these veterans could not be located and the money was in a dormant account and could be activated any time the veteran contacted the Veterans Administration.

The check that I had obtained from Cal was in the name of a veteran. However, the address was wrong. The veteran was not known there. Cal had arranged to send the check to that address and then was able to intercept it. It was agreed that I would pay Cal for the check he gave me. Then I would supply him with fifteen addresses in the New York area. (These addresses were actually the addresses of our own Secret Service agents who own homes and could arrange to get the checks even though they were in the name of other persons than what was on the mail box.) Arrangements were made to have a listening device in my hotel room and have officials of the Veterans Administration auditing department and general accounting office listen to our conversation in order to find out how Cal was able to pull this swindle.

Cal came to my hotel room and we immediately got into a conversation about the checks. I paid him for the check he gave me and then supplied him with the list of addresses he wanted. His only concern was that I would see to it that these checks were intercepted and not returned to the Government. He explained that if the checks were returned, it would not be fatal but it might cause some suspicion in his department. I assured him that I had arranged to get the checks and they would not be returned. He assured me again that there was no way of getting caught and that I could even put the check through my personal account as there would never be a complaint from the veteran. I asked him how he could be so sure that the veteran would not complain. He said he would explain it to me but he was sure that it was too complicated. I told him to go ahead as I had plenty of time to waste and beating the Government intrigued me.

He then explained a very complicated system whereby he would activate the dormant account, arrange to have a check sent by the Treasury Department to whatever address he wanted to use. He also was able to keep the account from having the money deducted from it. The auditors in the next room listened carefully and were able to follow him easier than I could. They later admitted that he had found a flaw in the system and could have bilked these dormant accounts out of untold thousands of dollars.

Cal told me to watch the mail carefully for the next ten days, that all the checks would be on their way within a week. We parted company and I promised to call him as soon as the checks were received. These particular checks were supposed to be all in the vicinity of one thousand dollars each.

About a week later, various agents in the office began to receive the checks at their home. Within ten days, all the checks were accounted for, exactly as Cal had predicted. It was planned that I would call Cal and tell him that most of the checks arrived and I had lookouts waiting for the remaining ones. I would then meet him at the hotel and tell him that I had cashed the checks that came. I would have a further conversation with him about the rest of the checks, supply him with a new list and then give a signal for the arrest.

Everything went along as planned. I met Cal in a local hotel, we went to my room where I told Cal that I was waiting for a courier to bring me the money for the checks. We had a further conversation about how long it would take for a new batch of checks to arrive. I gave him a list of about thirty more addresses. A knock came at the hotel door. I opened it and one man in the group announced that he was my parole officer that I had violated my parole by leaving the state. He immediately searched me and found a dozen Government checks in my possession. Cal almost fainted when he saw them extract the checks from my pocket. They asked him who he was and what he was doing in my hotel room. Cal stated he was a Government employee, that he was a friend of mine and he did not do anything wrong. I was advised that I was being returned to New York for parole violation and also would be charged with theft of the Government checks. At this point, I turned to Cal and told him that I was going to confess. I explained that I owed seven and a half years to the state and that I could not afford to be charged with the theft of the Government checks. I then turned to the police and stated that I had received these checks from Cal, that Cal was a Government employee and he had a way of getting these issued in any number and amounts. I told them that we were going to cash these checks and split the money. Cal turned pale and after some questioning, he finally told the whole story. I was supposedly returned to a New York prison and was quickly taken out of the picture.

Further questioning of Cal revealed that there were several other people employed by the Government who were involved with him. They were identified and arrested. After an exhaustive auditing, it appeared that Cal had just started on this scheme and not too many checks were sent out. The system was overhauled and further thefts were prevented. It was estimated that Cal could have bilked the accounts out of literally millions of dollars if the scheme had lasted for any length of time.

Because of his cooperation and the fact that he had no prior criminal record, Cal received a fairly light sentence and within a year and a half, he was back on the street. He stopped in to see the informant and asked about me. The informant stated that I was still in jail. Cal felt very sorry and periodically calls at the informant's place of business and leaves a carton of cigarettes for me.

Needless to say, Fred called me on many occasions thereafter and I always responded, even though he was not in my district. I took the time out to see him and made another attempt at an undercover case.

If the means of delivery cannot readily be ascertained, the informant and undercover agent should be questioned privately regarding their observations at the time the delivery was made. Very often the undercover agent will be able to tell about how the delivery was made, who made it and whether or not the person is in the immediate neighborhood. The evidence at the scene should be secured immediately. One agent should be in charge of the evidence so that the chain will not be broken. In other words, one agent obtains the evidence, initials it and puts it in a safe place in the office and brings it to court when it is needed. This will prevent the necessity of having several agents being called to court for the purpose of identifying the evidence and establishing the necessary chain.

In the event that the case is important enough, arrangements should be made to photograph the plant, if one has been seized. A photograph should be taken of the plant before it has been searched and after it has been searched to show the condition of the plant before and after the agents arrival and departure. The contraband seized at the scene should be counted, initialed and secured as soon as possible.

An undercover agent should be given an opportunity to make the notes necessary for his report. He should be given a private room, typewriter, etc. so he can make these notes while the events are still fresh in his mind.

Each officer and agent at the scene should be given a definite job such as transporting the contraband to the office, bringing the prisoners to a predesignated spot for questioning, and making a place available to the undercover agent and informant for questioning and reports. If this is not planned in advance, there will be much time lost at the scene of the arrest. All assignments should be carried out immediately and all agents should leave the scene as quickly as possible. The supervisor should make sure each officer at the scene prepares a report detailing exactly what he did and what he saw at the time the deal was being consummated. This again should be done as quickly as possible. If too much time is allowed to elapse, officers will be unnecessarily delayed in getting their reports into headquarters. It is the supervisors job to see that all reports are accurate and are received on time.

If a case is large enough, there are times when Assistant United States Attorneys or District Attorneys are given sufficient notice so they can be available immediately after the arrest to take care of the legal problems that might arise. Having an Assistant United States Attorney or District Attorney on the scene is very helpful and he can generally take part in the questioning of the suspects. He can make certain that the suspects are given all their rights.

Regardless of all the precautions that are taken to insure an undercover agent's safety, there are always the unforeseen events and situations that cannot possibly be predicted. We can choose an agent for undercover work in an area that he has never been before. He can be supplied with all the necessary cover, he can work with a tried and tested informant and still the case fails, sometimes even before it begins. On some occasions, the reason for the failures are obvious. These failures exist because the human element cannot be taken into consideration. There is always the possibility of the agent being recognized by someone whose presence could not have been included in the original planning.

Waxey Gordon was a racketeer of some note in the New York area. He had been arrested and convicted many times and he was the target of both the local and federal authorities in the New York area. He had a reputation of handling all kinds of contraband in large amounts. He was already a three time loser and had to be very careful about the next arrest because another conviction would mean that he would have to spend the rest of his natural life in jail.

I had just finished working an undercover case with an informant. This informant had many contacts in the underworld and he was anxious to make cases against all of them. He hoped to get enough money to leave the area and start a new life. The case we had just finished working was a large counterfeiting case and his reward was in the vicinity of $1,000. On this occasion, he asked me if I knew Waxey Gordon. I told him I only knew him by reputation; that I had never met him and I was positive Waxey did not know me. The informant stated that he had learned that Waxey was handling counterfeit money and he thought he could make arrangements for me to meet him. The informant suggested that at precisely 8:00 PM on the following Tuesday, I should make it my business to be at a mid-town bar. He stated that about that time, he would be with Waxey and several of Waxey's friends. He stated that he knew that at about 8:00 PM, on Tuesday evening, Waxey would go to this bar for a meeting with some of his associates. The plan was for me to sit at the end of the bar near the door to the back room. When Waxey, his friends and the informant came in, the informant would recognize me as an old friend that he had not seen in years. He would then introduce me to Waxey and the others and invite me in the back room. He would indicate to Waxey that I was a person who could dispose of any kind of contraband. He stated he was sure that Waxey would then offer me either narcotics or counterfeit money. Everything was set for that night and about 7:30 PM I entered the bar at the far end and ordered a drink.

Shortly after I had arrived, a man entered the bar. He was obviously intoxicated. When I got a good look at him, my heart sank as I recognized him as a former sergeant in the Marine Corps who served under me overseas. He came from Missouri and I was at a loss to figure out what he was doing in this part of the country. I hoped he would not see me as he was a "loud mouth" even when he was sober. Sure enough, he surveyed each and every person at the bar and when he saw me, he immediately waved his hand and shouted, "Hi, Captain." At first I paid no attention to him but his loud shouts were obviously aimed at me and I waved back to him indicating recognition. He then left his spot at the bar and staggered over to me. When he got close he said, "remember me, Captain"? I answered that he looked familiar. He immediately laughed and shouted in a loud voice, "isn't it your business to recognize people. You are supposed to be the best damned federal agent in the country. You must be working undercover or something." At this point, everyone left the bar in a hurry, leaving the good sergeant and myself there alone. There was nothing left to do but drag the sergeant out of the bar and get away in a hurry.

Shortly after we left, I saw the informant together with Waxey and his associates enter the bar. I made no attempt to contact the informant.

The following day, he called me. He told me that it was a good thing that I did not meet him the night before. He stated that when he went into the bar, the bartender told Waxey that the place was surrounded with federal agents and there was going to be trouble. He said one of the agents posed as a drunk and he was sure that they were still in the area. The informant stated that Waxey and his friends were quite alarmed and left the place immediately. I told the informant that I too had noticed a lot of law in the vicinity and decided not to keep the appointment. I blew the only opportunity I had to make a case against Waxey.

I made several mistakes that night. The first one was in not grabbing the sergeant as soon as he entered the bar and explaining why he should not be there. The second mistake was in taking a chance coming early for the appointment and putting myself on display for an extra half hour. Perhaps it was best that it ended that way. I could have entered there on time and have been introduced to Waxey and his friends, then the sergeant could have come into the bar and there would have been trouble.

Nothing was really lost, because shortly thereafter, Waxey was

officers, allowing a suspect to draw a revolver, all can contribute to bedlam at the time of an arrest. Before discussing the arrest, perhaps it would be beneficial to talk about what we should prepare for in the briefing prior to the buy and arrest.

In cases involving large amounts of money or involving important violators, we have found that a surveillance vehicle is of the utmost importance. This vehicle, in the form of a nondescript truck, a taxi cab, a bus or station wagon can allow the surveilling officers to get close to the scene of the action and at the same time obtain a maximum amount of cover. In surveillance trucks, pictures can be taken and enough personnel can be hidden in the truck to take care of any emergency that might occur. Of course, with a surveillance vehicle, there comes a certain amount of responsibility. This vehicle should not be unmasked except in an emergency. Routine arrests should not be made from the surveillance truck. The reason being that word will soon get around that the police are using unmarked special trucks. The description of these vehicles would soon be revealed. However, in an emergency, the identity of the vehicle is secondary to aiding an officer in making an arrest or saving the life of someone.

Another typically obvious police vehicle should be in the vicinity, one in which a red light can be uncovered and used, equipped with siren and other articles used in police vehicles, such as first aid kits, radios, ropes, ladders and other tools of the trade.

In doing undercover work, the officers are now using cars which not only do not look like police vehicles but cars that could stand minute inspection by the suspects. At the time of the arrest, the police vehicle should be in a position to move in closely so that they can notify local police officers that an arrest is in progress. Generally in an arrest there should be two groups, an inner perimeter and an outer perimeter. The inner perimeter are agents or police who will be directly concerned with the actual arrest of the suspects. The outer perimeter will act as a reserve. They will notify the local police who appear on the scene that an arrest is taking place and they will look for other escaping suspects and people involved in the crime that is not obvious to the arresting officers. These officers should be dressed in business clothes and should be in a position to identify themselves as officers immediately when the arrest is in progress. All officers involved in the arrest, inner or outer perimeter, should place their shields on their persons as soon as practical, so there is no doubt as to who the officers are. Wherever practical, a member of the local police force should be on the scene at the time of a contemplated arrest. Out of necessity, he would be in the outer perimeter because he will probably be recognized if he is too close to the transaction. The local officer should be teamed with a member of the agency who is controlling the case. These officers, in the outer perimeter, will be in a position to identify fellow officers who may stumble on the scene at the time of an arrest or shootout. Arrangements should be made for as much radio contact as possible.

The above are some of the things that should be given some thought before the actual arrest takes place. Before we can discuss how a physical arrest is to be made, we have to explore the manner in which the undercover case is being handled and how it is expected to end.

Let us say that it has been agreed that a buy will take place in a hotel or motel room. The undercover agent has arranged with the suspect that it will be a hand-to-hand delivery in the room. The suspect, at the appointed time, is observed entering the lobby of the hotel or motel. Covering agents in the outer perimeter should immediately relay the information to the agents in the inner perimeter. The inner perimeter in this case would probably be agents who are in an adjoining room to where the buy is to take place. They should be notified that the suspect has arrived, the method of arrival, how many are involved, a complete description of the suspect, and if it is obvious that he is carrying contraband. It is rarely obvious that the suspect is actually carrying contraband. However, he may be observed carrying a suitcase, a cardboard box, or a large wrapped package. This does not mean that the package actually contains contraband. It may be a lure to trigger a premature arrest. This is a device used many times in the past. Under no circumstances should an agent feel that the suspect is actually carrying contraband and effect his arrest. This case must proceed as planned and be allowed to run its course. A suitcase full of old telephone books is a poor substitute for a large amount of any contraband at the termination of the case.

After the suspect proceeds to the lobby or the room of the undercover agents, a listening device will generally alert the agents as to whether or not a bona fide delivery is taking place. If the delivery has taken place, the undercover agent must be in a position to make the payment. He generally will not admit that he has the buy money in the room (he is afraid of a stick-up). He will either send another agent to pick up the money while the suspect waits in the room with the contraband, or he will go himself to a safe at the desk where he has left a package. He will either be accompanied by the suspect or he will go alone. Perhaps the suspect will have a partner to accompany the agent while the original suspect stays with the contraband. If the suspects separate during the transaction, the arrest can be effected as follows. After the signal has been given that a delivery has been made, the inner perimeter agents can enter the agent's room either by an adjoining door or can enter by using a key which had been obtained in advance. The subject in the room can be placed under arrest and the outer perimeter agents have been advised that an arrest took place in the hotel room. If another arrest is to take place at the desk in the lobby, the outer perimeter agents can effect this arrest quietly at the desk. An agent and local detective should be nearby to advise any local police that an arrest is taking place and also to help the arresting officers, if necessary. In the event there is trouble, a car outside should put its lights on (red turning). This will signal local police in the area that something is going on involving police. The surveillance truck in the vicinity has been there for some time. If they have seen anything that needs attention, the men inside this vehicle can take care of it. During all these phases, radio contact must be made with the command post (this generally will be in the hotel in another nearby room).

There are times in various cities where the agents are friendly with the owners or employees of hotels and motels. There are times when these people can be taken into our confidence in order to get the proper rooms and cover. As long as the hotel or motel does not get any undue publicity, very often they will cooperate with some authorities. Each case should be handled on its own merits. No undue chances should be taken. At the time of an arrest, agents should put on their shields in full view so as not to be mistaken for one of the violators.

Very often the suspect will not agree to a hotel or motel room, perhaps he has had previous experience with a buy that went wrong for either himself or one of his accomplices. This type of person will want to proceed as cautiously as he can. Generally, it will be too safe and the agent can turn down his suggestions because it would leave the agent and his "buy money" in an exposed position. If the agent is posing as someone from out of town, it can be suggested that the airport be the place of delivery. The agent argues that just as soon as he gets his delivery, he wants to leave as quickly as possible and get the contraband back to his people. The agent can give the suspect a general idea of the time he will arrive, without mentioning the flight number and the exact time of arrival. If these arrangements are agreeable to the suspect, the agent can also indicate that he will leave the buy money in a locker box at the airport so that he can pay for the contraband as soon as the delivery takes place. The inner perimeter in this case can cover the vicinity of the locker box where the agent has placed his money. They know full well that the agent will not take the suspect to the box nor will he open it unless he has seen the notes or has actually taken possession of the contraband. When the buy money is being retrieved from the locker box, this generally will be the signal for the arrest. The agents in the inner perimeter can take the suspect into custody. The outer perimeter will be on the alert for any accomplices that they might have noticed in the background, also they will be on the alert for any police who may be alerted by the arrest. At this time, agents from the police car and or surveillance vehicle can seize any vehicle that the suspect might have used. They can also line up the necessary vehicles to take the suspects away from the scene. This should be done as expeditiously as possible. The less people who know about the arrest, the better. One agent should take custody of the contraband and keep custody of it so there will be no trouble in entering it as evidence at the time of the trial. About the same procedure can be worked for a railroad station and bus terminal if no airport is available. There will be very little variation in these types of cases except that the subject may want to make the transfer in a car in the parking lot. This will not create a problem as the undercover agent will have to go to the locker box to get his money. He should have seen the contraband and the agents from the outer perimeter should be in a position to cover the transaction while the agents in the inner perimeter make the necessary changes.

There are times when the subject insists upon making a deal at a restaurant on a busy turnpike or highway. This will necessitate the using of cars by both the suspect and the undercover agent. Generally, the suspect will get to the restaurant early and look it over. He will also make a pass at the parking lot to see if there are any people just sitting in cars. He will then meet the agent in the restaurant or bar and have a conversation. He will either have the contraband with him or he will be expecting a delivery. The undercover agent in this case tells the suspect that he is ready to go and the money is locked in his car. The suspect will either have the contraband in his car or will go to the parking lot and obtain it from an accomplice. The outer perimeter, of course, is either in the parking lot or close by where the lot can be kept under surveillance. The surveillance vehicle will come in handy if heavier vehicles are allowed on the parkway or turnpike. Here again, it must be remembered that nothing can happen until the agent goes to get his money. The outer perimeter will cover the agent while getting his money. If the suspect is with him, both will be placed under arrest in the lot. The agents in the restaurant who were in the inner perimeter will leave the restaurant and lend assistance to the arresting agents, and carry on the normal functions of the outer perimeter.

Very often the suspect will insist on making a deal at a large shopping center. Here the agent can control the activity by again using a car and keeping the buy money in the car. Whatever contact he has with the suspect can be loosely followed by agents of the inner perimeter and the official car can be covered by agents of the outer perimeter. In an area such as this, a surveillance vehicle will come in handy as there are generally many trucks making deliveries in the area. After the agent has seen the notes or accepted delivery from the suspect, he will go to his car and get his money from the trunk or wherever it has been placed. This signal will notify all agents that the undercover agent is ready for an arrest. Again, agents from the inner perimeter can effect the arrest of the suspects while the undercover agent can be taken in custody by an agent of the outer perimeter. Other agents will act as reserve and be in a position to notify local police etc., of what is going on.

We have seen times when the suspect insists on doing business either in his home or an apartment that he has the keys for. Again, if this is a substantial purchase, the undercover agent can go to this home or apartment, but insists that he will not bring his money there because he does not know what to expect when he gets there. When he sees the contraband or gets the delivery he can ask the suspect to accompany him to his car. When he goes to the car and gives the signal, the arrest can be effected on the street. One group for the arrest and the other to search the apartment or home. In all of the above cases, once the signal is given, no time should be lost in effecting the arrest. A few seconds could make the difference between success and failure. If the suspect is armed, the loss of a few seconds can trigger off a series of events which could be disastrous.

Another method of delivery can be car to car. The suspect arranges to meet the undercover agent in a certain neighborhood and tells him to park his car at a certain location. He then will cruise the area before delivery to make sure that there are no suspicious cars or persons in the vicinity. It is very important in cases such as these to use a surveillance vehicle to get the maximum amount of cover for the agents who are to make the arrest.

PUBLICITY

A successful case usually ends with an arrest and a sizeable seizure of contraband. This type of case is newsworthy and of much interest to the press. Whether or not to allow publicity is a problem that faces each agency after a successful case. Unfortunately, publicity is an important adjunct of police work. Most agencies have a never-ending battle with the budget and in order to obtain a workable budget, the agency must get favorable publicity on the work they are doing. The various legislators (City, State or Federal) generally hold hearings in order to determine the size of the budget they will allow for enforcement work. The administrators of the police agencies must be armed with statistics that will help them obtain the funds they need to wage a successful war against crime. The publicity that the department gets is remembered by the legislators and they are undoubtedly influenced by what they read in the press.

The police must decide whether or not to meet the press and issue a release at the conclusion of a successful case. To give the press the facts as they happened will tend to expose the informant. To mention that it was an undercover case will indicate that there was an undercover agent involved and this will alert the defendants that they were "set up" and again the informant will be in jeopardy. To try to distort the facts to the press is undesirable and dangerous. Most reporters are familiar with the workings of an undercover case and if they feel that they are being "thrown a curve" they will dig deeper into the facts in order to get at the truth.

Time is an important factor and it is something that most police departments desperately need in trying to continue on with a long investigation, especially if it involves undercover work. One phase of the case may be finished but there may be other phases that need further investigation. If all the facts are published in the press the case can be ruined. Reporters realize that undercover work provides interesting reading and interesting reading sells papers. However, the premature publishing of the facts of a case can do irreparable harm to the investigation. The only alternative the agency has is to completely ignore the press and thereby cause their displeasure. This is a sure way to get adverse publicity. There are some areas where the police and press have a good working relationship and the press will cooperate by printing only that which will not jeopardize the informant or the outcome of the case. There are some investigations, however, where all the facts can be given to the press when the investigation ends. In these cases, there generally are no informants involved and the police can feel free to answer most of the questions asked by the press. There are not many choices offered in handling the press and a decision is difficult to arrive at.

Chapter 5

APATHY

I F I were asked to name the one attitude which does not belong in any police department, it would be "apathy." Apathy takes many forms in investigative work: the unwillingness to take an honest gamble, the fear of "rocking the boat," the desire to just work on the big case and avoid the small one, and the unwillingness to take on the slightest responsibility. The young officer as well as the old timers are equally guilty of being apathetic. There are many old timers who have "put in their time" and do not want to become involved in anything more than the most routine of matters. It can be said that they are "retired on full pay." There are also some young officers who are so preoccupied with studying for promotion and for degrees in higher education that they do not seem to have the time for the duties for which they are being paid. There are some investigators who constantly shift around and try to pick out the "big ones" which might bring instant recognition or some other form of reward. The small case that has been kicked aside could possibly be just as rewarding to the officer, perhaps not in the form of monetary gain or departmental recognition, but just knowing that the job was done right and the honest effort paid off. The "big one" may never come along but any number of the small ones, if worked properly, can lead to the big one. When police work becomes dull and routine and the desire to solve the case is no longer there, then it is time for the officer or investigator to seek other employment. Police work is not the best paying work today but many of us in it get a sense of fulfillment in trying to prevent crime and arrest violators. A good example of putting maximum effort in a small case which paid off is the case of "The Spider."

The Spider was a young lad who had more than his share of "brushes with the law." He had never served any real time. However, his several arrests had given him a bad reputation in the neighborhood. He had long forgotten what it was like to have a decent family life. He was orphaned at an early age and had escaped from all the homes he had been placed in.

One day, The Spider had been identified as the passer of a new counterfeit twenty dollar bill. He was picked up by the police and then turned over to the Secret Service for further questioning and prosecution. The Spider maintained that he had found several bills on the street, that he did not know they were counterfeit and passed them. The Spider would normally be considered just another passer. He would be questioned and either released or arraigned. What made The Spider important in this case was the fact that he was the only one who had access to these notes. The notes were new, they were of excellent quality and no others had appeared in circulation. We felt The Spider was either in a position to steal the notes or he had access to where they were being printed. We felt sure that The Spider had enough information which would help us to capture the plant before the notes were extensively distributed. While questioning The Spider, word had come to us that another police department felt that The Spider was a suspect in connection with the murder of a taxi cab driver. The police wanted an opportunity to do some background work on him and then wanted him made available at a later date for questioning about this homicide.

After spending several hours with The Spider, I felt that he was putting on a big front but down deep he was just a scared kid and if we could press the right button, he might go along with us and cooperate. There were times during the questioning when it appeared that he might bend a little but just as soon as he was pressed for pertinent information, he would "clam up." There was no problem in getting him to admit that he had passed the counterfeit notes. This was not the issue. The problem was to shake his story that he found the notes in the street. The Spider was about eighteen years of age and had a soft spot for a girl who lived in the neighborhood who was physically handicapped. The thought of being separated from her for a period of time seemed to worry him. I was able to get permission from the United States Attorney's office to get a quick arraignment on The Spider just before the court closed. We wanted to be sure that The Spider was arraigned, released on his own recognizance and try to arrange not to have any publicity. We knew The Spider was not newsworthy as he was being arraigned for passing one counterfeit note and we hoped that it would not be reported in the press. After the arraignment, I decided to take a chance and hope that The Spider would talk to us after he was released. He agreed to come back to the office after the court proceedings to discuss the case. Of course, he could stand on his Constitutional rights and refuse to have anything to do with us and he was perfectly free to go back to his source and let the source know he was arrested.

When we arrived at the office, The Spider was again advised that he could terminate the questioning at any time and he was free to go home. His attitude began to change and for the first time he felt that he could trust someone. We spent quite some time on small talk, we ate and then got back on the subject of counterfeit notes. At one point, he stated that he did not want to go any further with the questioning. He got up and started to leave the office. No one stopped him and he got as far as the door and he decided to come back. This appeared to be a test to see if he was actually free to go when he pleased.

He sat down and announced that he was ready to tell the whole story. Again, he asked if he was still free to go home. He was advised that he would go home regardless of what he said. He then told us of getting a job in a print shop several months before in the neighborhood where he lived. He stated he did odd jobs around the shop and ran errands for the owner, whom we shall call George. George was no ordinary printer. He was a third generation printer and engraver. He knew lithography, photography and all the allied arts. A few weeks after he started working for him, The Spider noticed that George was experimenting with making counterfeit notes. The Spider happened to come into the shop after hours and saw evidence of counterfeiting. The Spider confronted George with the evidence he found and George promised to make The Spider a partner in the counterfeiting activities. George continued with his experimenting but never seemed satisfied with his work. The Spider managed to steal several of the experimental notes before they were destroyed and this was the cause of his present predicament. The Spider stated that he did not have any problem passing the notes and denied that there were any more left. He stated that George always destroyed the negatives, the plates and the notes when he completed his experiments. The Spider went on to say that on several occasions he helped George destroy thousands of dollars in counterfeit money that George felt was not good enough to pass. The Spider assured us that George's shop was absolutely clean and it would do us no good to get a search warrant. There was no way of telling when George would start up again. The Spider knew George was under financial pressure and was getting visits from several characters who wanted George to make counterfeit money and counterfeit checks, to pay off some debts. The counterfeits made by George were of excellent quality but George was a perfectionist and was never satisfied with his finished product. We did not want to expose The Spider by using him as a witness against George. It would be a weak case at best and our only chance was to gamble with The Spider and trust him to keep us advised as to George's counterfeiting activities.

The Spider seemed to enjoy the prospect of working undercover for the Government. He promised to go back to his job in the shop and report several times a week. Surprisingly, The Spider was prompt and accurate in his reporting. He gave us the names and license numbers of the shady characters that visited George and he reported on George's movements and the conversations he had with him. George had plenty of legitimate business to keep him going and he postponed his counterfeit activities until he had more time to spare.

While we were waiting for George to get started again, we found time during the lull to let the police question The Spider about the homicide (the suspected connection with the murder of the taxi cab driver). The Spider cooperated with the police, answered all questions and was subsequently cleared of any complicity in the crime. For the first time in his young life, The Spider was seeing daylight and he liked the idea of not running away from every policeman he came in contact with. He continued making his reports. On his visits to our office he joined in small talk with some of the agents, he had breakfast with us two or three times a week and even borrowed money on a payday-to-payday basis. He was as prompt with paying his loans as he was with his reporting. The Spider began to go to the dentist to take care of his teeth. He bought himself some new clothes, got a part-time job and started dating Edna, his handicapped girl friend. So it went for four, five, six, seven and eight months. We began to wonder if George was tipped off or The Spider had double crossed us. I took a lot of "good natured riding" from some of the personnel in the office. A lot of them felt that The Spider was bad all the way through and should not have been trusted. I still felt he was leveling with us. No new notes were appearing and it was obvious that George was not back in the counterfeiting business. Surveillance on George's printing shop did not indicate that George was engaged in any illegal activities.

Finally, one day The Spider reported that George was talking about making one hundred dollar bills. George had stated that he had developed a new process for making counterfeit notes and he was sure that he could make a very deceptive bill. He began buying supplies and working a little bit at the end of each working day. The Spider was allowed to stay around while George worked on making the plates. After several weeks, George announced that the plates were finished and he was thoroughly satisfied with the way they turned out. He told The Spider that he had large orders for these counterfeit bills and that very shortly he would start printing.

The Spider was now reporting several times daily and one day he told us that George was going to start printing on a Thursday night. We wanted to obtain a search warrant for the premises but did not want to use The Spider as the witness. The printing shop was on the street level and was easy to cover but the windows were painted black and we could not see into the plant. The night before the printing started, The Spider made sure that enough paint was scrapped from the window to give us a clear view of George's activities. George meticulously followed his schedule. He started printing in the late afternoon on a Thursday and planned to stay in his shop all weekend, if necessary, until the job was finished. On Thursday we observed George at the machine printing the notes. Based on what we had seen, we were able to get a search warrant.

The following day, we went into the shop while George was printing the counterfeit one hundred dollar bills. The Spider had not shown up and was not on the premises when the arrest was made. George turned out to be an extremely intelligent individual and was tops in the printing trade and could have made a good living by working legitimately. He apparently got carried away with his own printing ability and wanted to go into competition with the Bureau of Engraving and Printing. Several hundred thousand dollars in finished notes were seized from the plant as well as George's press, camera and other equipment used in manufacturing the notes. George indicated he was going to fight the case but after speaking with an attorney, he decided to cooperate and go along with the Government in identifying and testifying against the others who were with him in his previous counterfeiting activities. The others were subsequently identified, arrested and convicted. For his cooperation, George received a suspended sentence and was placed on probation. He later became a good friend of the Service as he had stayed in the trade and was responsible for helping us with several major cases. George married, bought a home in another part of the country, has a growing family and a successful business. The last time I talked with him, he told me he was going to write a book. It is hoped that it will be a textbook on printing.

What about The Spider? He also received a suspended sentence. He married Edna, moved away, went into a plumbing business and is raising a family. He has had no trouble since the day we picked him up for passing the counterfeit note.

This case could not have worked out better. It was a gamble that paid off and I hate to think of how many that went the other way, especially those cases that died and we could never be sure that our trust was misplaced or something unforeseen "tipped the scales" against us. When all the facts are analyzed, we do not have too much choice in the matter. We could have thrown The Spider in jail and held him in high bail. George would eventually learn of The Spider's arrest and would have undoubtedly been more careful and perhaps would have dropped The Spider entirely as being "too hot." If we trusted The Spider and he turned against us, he would have to admit to George that he was picked up and released. Either way, we would have lost. So it all boiled down to the fact that there were very few alternatives. The right choice was made and it paid off. It would be folly to think that all of the cases where we trust someone would end as well as this one. All we can do is play with the possibilities and take the one which we think has the best chance of being successful. The principal thing to remember is "do something." You can never be sure if a plan will work unless it is tried. It was refreshing to note that in this case all the personnel involved was enthusiastic about its possibilities. Long hours were involved and there were many headaches but nowhere in the case did apathy rear its ugly head. I have to admit that George's work was the best I have ever seen. The effort that went into this case paid off handsomely. If George's counterfeiting activites were not curtailed early in his career, the public would have been victimized by untold thousands of dollars in these counterfeit notes.

Figure 13. Counterfeit money recovered from trash barrel of print shop.

Chapter 6

QUESTIONS AND ANSWERS

During my years with the Federal Government, I have spent much time preparing younger agents for undercover assignments. In connection with teaching at not only the United States Secret Service but other police academies, there are always good questions asked by the students. I have kept track of the better questions and have set forth in this chapter the answers I have given them.

Q: Should a police officer or agent be armed while doing undercover work?

A: Unfortunately, undercover work is not an exact science. Each case is different and must be judged on its own merits. The question of whether or not an undercover agent should be armed while doing undercover work will change depending on the circumstances of the particular case. I have never carried a gun while working undercover but this certainly is not a criteria by which each case should be judged. I had always felt that it would be difficult to explain to a suspect why I was carrying a gun. I also felt that in the event that something went wrong, I might not be given an opportunity to use it. This again, however, is personal. I feel that anyone working undercover should carry a gun if he feels the need to. This should override all other conditions. If an agent has no particular thoughts about it, the superior officer in charge can consider various factors like who the suspects are, the amount of danger involved, how well can the agent be covered while he is actually working, is there any chance for gun play in the case. In the event there is an element of danger, the supervisor will suggest to the undercover man that he be armed. It is not necessary, of course, to carry the official revolver. A small gun which can be easily concealed is more advisable.

Q: Should an agent be covered at all times while working in an undercover capacity?

A: This can only be answered in the same way as the preceding question. An agent working undercover in a "buy" situation should be covered at all times, especially if an arrest is imminent. There are times, however, when undercover agents have to accompany suspects on short trips either to pick up the contraband or to meet the other violators. Sometimes it is not practical to follow the agent and the suspect when they leave the scene. Arrangements should be made in advance for the agent to make contact with his superior as soon as it is practical so that he can advise where he is and the surveillance can be taken up at that point. If an agent is working on long-term, intelligence-seeking assignments, there are times when he will be out of contact for long periods of time. Here again, arrangements are made in advance for the method to be used by the agent to contact his superiors. To boil it all down, wherever practicable, an agent working undercover should be kept under surveillance by his fellow agents to render assistance in the event that he needs it. The case should be controlled in such a manner, that there will be no problems in covering the agent.

An example including both situations of whether an agent should be armed or whether an agent should be covered at all times while working undercover is as follows.

I had just finished an assignment in Philadelphia, Pennsylvania, and was departing the office to go back to New York when a telephone call was received at the office from an informant who stated that he had been propositioned to purchase counterfeit notes and was in a position to obtain a sample. The informant was tending bar in a town that I would have to pass through on my way back to New York. Since I knew that I would be assigned to do the undercover work in the case, I volunteered to stop by on my way home to see the informant and find out if a case could be developed. The informant was running a small bar on the outskirts of a town near the turnpike.

I stopped in to see him and after introducing myself to him he told me that a patron of the bar had a sample of a counterfeit note and wanted to sell the notes in large quantities. While we were talking, the suspect walked into the bar and the bartender introduced me to him as a friend from New York. The suspect and I engaged in small talk for the next hour or so. He then got on the subject of various types of contraband and he showed me a sample of counterfeit money that his group was selling. He asked me if I was interested in making a purchase. I told him that I was not in a position to make a large purchase at that time but that I could invest several hundred dollars in some notes, bring them to New York and come back with a larger order. He asked me to stay around for a while and perhaps he could arrange for me to meet his friends. The hour was fairly late and there was no way that I could make contact with the office.

At about the time the bar was ready to close, the suspect and I walked out the back parking lot where there were two men waiting in a car. I was invited in the car and a conversation soon ensued about counterfeit money. The driver of the car became suspicious of me and started to ask a lot of questions. I apparently was not giving him the correct answers and he was becoming annoyed with me. He was armed and his friend was also armed. The suspect stated that if he though I was "wrong" he would have no compunction about killing me and dropping my body in the nearby river. Both his friends agreed with him and at that time the situation became extremely tight. He continued to ask me questions and I finally told him that I was in the dress business in New York. He stated that he had good connections in the dress business and asked me the name of my employer. I picked at random the name of a dress manufacturer in New York, knowing full well that he was not in a position to contact this person at that time. He went through some of the motions about making telephone calls and checking me out. For some reason, they decided to let me go and released me from the car at about 4:00 in the morning.

At a later date, a case was made against all these individuals and at this time it was learned from one of them that on the particular night in question, they were very serious about killing the man who they had in the car as they suspected he might be an informant or an undercover agent.

The working of this case without cover was very foolish on my part. It was one of the rare times when the office had no idea of where I was or what I was doing other than the fact that I mentioned I was going to talk to an informant. It would have been far better had I been kept under surveillance because covering my meeting with these people would have provided the government with several more witnesses needed to corroborate the testimony I gave in court after the defendants were arrested. It was very hard for a jury to believe that a man would be working undercover and that there were no other agents in sight. The question of whether it would have been better to be armed at that time is problematical. Perhaps if I were armed and drew a revolver, during the discussion, it might have caused a shootout as at least two of the other people were armed and someone might have been unnecessarily killed.

Q: How much should an undercover agent tell his family when he is on an assignment?

A: The families of most undercover agents have accepted the fact that their husbands or relatives work undercover, and there is a certain amount of danger connected with their work. Most undercover agents advise their families at an early date that they are working undercover, they will receive strange telephone calls, they will go out at very odd hours and they will be seen in the company of some very strange people. The wife and family of the agent must accept this or the peace and tranquility of the home will be spoiled at an early date. If the family accepts this, it is not necessary to give them a day by day report on the status of the case. Very often, the very life of the undercover agent depends upon the facts in the case remaining confidential until a certain phase of the case is reached, giving too much information even to one's family might be dangerous and not only spoil the case but put the agent in a perilous position.

Q: What should an agent do if he is riding in a car with a suspect and the suspect "makes a tail"?

A: Very often the suspect will mention to the agent that he thinks he is being tailed. He will then test to see if the car behind him is actually following him. He will do this by stopping, double parking, turning into a one-way street, speeding, jumping a light or anything else that may come to his mind at the time. If it is obvious to the agent that they are, in fact, being followed, the agent should agree with the suspect that there is a tail. He then should request the suspect to drop him off as quickly as possible because he feels he is not in a position to be questioned by the police either because he is carrying contraband or because he is on parole. Being on parole would be dangerous to him if he were caught in the company of people with criminal records. Any excuse will generally be acceptable. Under no condition should he insist that they are not being tailed. This would tend to make the suspect suspicious of the agent.

Q: Is it a good idea to try and meet a suspect without the use of an informant?

A: Yes, if it can be done it is a good idea. I find it is almost impossible to meet the suspect without an informant unless the undercover agent spends a long time in the area where the suspects are known to operate. In most of our cases, we do not have the time or manpower to invest in a case that may bring nebulous results. In the event it can be done, a lot of headaches are saved in trying to protect and safeguard the informant.

I can recall a case where I was to meet a suspect in the lobby of a motel at a certain hour. The case was in the mid-west and the informant was being handled by someone else. When I arrived in the city, someone had the time element all fouled up. The suspect was to arrive at the motel looking for me at 2:00 PM. I could just barely make it by 1:00 PM. The informant was also to arrive at the motel at 2:00 PM. All I knew was that the informant had told the suspect that my name was Felix Marlowe.

When I arrived at the motel, I found that Felix Marlowe was being paged. I also learned that the suspect was in the bar waiting for me and the informant. I did not know the informant nor the suspect, so I went to the bar and asked for the man that was paging Felix Marlowe. The bartender pointed out a man called Alex. I went over to Alex and introduced myself to him. We had a short conversation (very guarded) on both sides. Finally, after ten minutes the informant arrived at the bar. I only knew him from the description previously given to me. I met him halfway across the room and was able to tell him who I was, out of earshot of the suspect. The informant was quite upset but came along all right after all of us had a few drinks at the bar. The prospect of making a case did not seem too good.

This case was fouled up from the beginning. However, it is

interesting to carry it along to see how it came out. The suspect in this case had excellent connections in spite of the fact that he was a cheap thug. All of the dealers in this particular counterfeit note made sure that enough money was advanced by any distributor so that the people who controlled the distribution would not lose anything in the event of a stickup or an arrest.

The conversation at the bar dealt with the delivery of fifty thousand dollars in counterfeit currency. This was no problem to Alex except that he wanted the "buy money" in advance. I told him I could not do that because the people who controlled the good money would hold me responsible in the event anything went wrong. I told him that if the money was mine I would be inclined to trust him, but I could not gamble with anyone else's money. We argued for about an hour and a half but could not come to any terms. I told him to forget the whole matter; that I was going back to New York the following morning and perhaps I would come back another time when I had my own money and we could do business on better terms. We parted company and I and several other agents got rooms at the motel that night. I registered under the name of Felix Marlowe and about 1:00 AM I went to bed.

About 3:30 AM, there was a knock at the door. I asked who it was and it was Alex. I asked him what he wanted and he said, "let me in, I have something for you." I was in no position to make a buy at that time. I did not have the genuine money nor did I have a gun, and there were no agents available to make the arrest. I was also not sure if he was trying to stick me up for the money he thought I had. I told him I would meet him in the lobby after I got dressed. He became very excited and wanted to know if I was crazy. He insisted that he had something and this was no time to play games. No matter what I told him, he would not go away. I stalled by saying I was getting dressed. He again became very annoyed wanting to know why I had to get dressed before opening the door. In the meantime, I got on the house phone and was able to locate a couple of agents in the motel who had rooms nearby. I told them to get in the hallway as soon as possible as I was about to let Alex in my room and I did not know if it was a delivery or a stickup.

I waited a few more minutes then opened the door. Alex was

one "mad hombre." He drew back his coat and took a large package of counterfeit hundred dollar bills from his back pockets. While he was still swearing and calling me all kinds of names I saw the agents approaching from down the hall and told Alex, "wait one second and I'll get the money." I motioned the agents to go into the room. They did and effected the arrest.

This particular case was really fouled up from the beginning. However, for some reason it was destined to work out and no matter how badly things were handled, it worked out. Frankly, I never expected Alex to return. I never thought he would unexpectedly come to my room for a delivery and I never thought he could get the merchandise without paying for it. I later learned that he really went overboard to convince the people to give him the money on consignment. He opened up old sores, of how he kept his mouth shut on previous arrests, how his family was not properly handled when he was serving time, he told of how the buyer was related to him and that he knew that this relative had all the money necessary to make the purchase. He put himself "out on a limb" and could never explain why it was necessary for him to lie about the buyer being a relative.

Q: Is it a good idea to meet the informant other than at the federal office or courthouse or police station?

A: Most of the time, the informant will tell you where he would like to meet you. On the surface it might be safe to say that an informant should always be met a long way from the official headquarters. However, there are times when there is no danger in the informant meeting the agent at the office. There are many factors that have to be taken into consideration. Do the informant and his friends come from the same city where their headquarters are? Would the informant normally have legitimate business in that particular building. Sometimes, the informant has an arrest pending and he would naturally be called to a courthouse on various occasions. It would suffice to say that this question would best be answered by the informant and he should be asked on the first contact if he has any objection to coming to headquarters.

I recall one informant who knew he was being followed by some of his friends. However, he went straight to the Federal Building in New York City and went to another agency where he

Figure 14. Author working undercover — meeting suspects prior to the delivery of counterfeits. Photo taken from surveillance truck.

had an arrest pending. When he left the building, he made a point of seeing his friends on the street and he let them know that this agency wanted him to cooperate with them. He said he was being harassed and he did not want them coming to his home, so he always came to the Federal Building whenever they wanted to see him. This took care of all the trips that he made to the Federal Building and he never worried about being followed anymore. I cannot say whether or not this was a good idea. However, it worked and the informant went on to make cases for several agencies thereafter.

In another case the informant was so high up in the underworld that it would have been sheer folly to have him come to the Federal Building. Elaborate plans were made to see this man miles and miles away from New York City and its environs. As time went on, he was becoming more and more sloppy about where he would meet the federal agents. He finally went into business and made the back of his store the meeting place for all the agencies he was cooperating with. No amount of cautioning could convince him that it was dangerous to have meetings on his premises. He was positive that he could talk himself out of any situation and he feared no one.

One day three men went into his place of business and emptied their revolvers into his head and left as quickly as they arrived. Again, perhaps this was meant to be but it is a good example where an informant was his own worst enemy. This man did not inform because he was a good citizen, he was faced with a fifteen year sentence that he was able to have reduced to probation. This again was dangerous but he insisted upon "calling his own shots" and eventually the shots proved his undoing.

Q: How close should an agent get with an informant?

A: This is a difficult question. It depends on the informant. Why he is informing and what he expects in return. If an informant has knowledge about many crimes other than the ones under the jurisdiction of the agency to which he is reporting, it is important that he be seen often in an effort to get the information on other crimes which could easily be more important than the ones he is reporting to you.

I do not want to be considered naive about cooperation.

However, I feel very strongly that all agencies should cooperate to the fullest and make information supplied by informants known to the agency that maintains the jurisdiction. Unfortunately, this is not always the case. Some agencies only question the informant about their own work and wink at the other violations. It is not necessary to make the informant available to the other agency, but the information definitely should be given. If the informant does not want to work with the other agency, he should be questioned and the information turned over to the other agency. If, on the other hand, the informant has no objection to working with the other agency, he should be introduced to one of their agents and be allowed to work for them. If the informant will not work with anyone except the agent who is handling him, this can be explained to the other agency. Very often the original undercover agent can work for both agencies. This has been done many times in the past when intelligent professional supervisors get together and "cut the red tape" that inevitably occurs when two law enforcement agencies try to work together.

There are times when, during the course of an investigation, an officer stumbles on information that may be of no value to him but can be extremely valuable to another agency. I would hate to think that there are officers who do not relay this information on to the proper agency. It is only through the combined efforts of all law enforcement personnel that the fight against crime can be effective.

About ten years ago I worked a simple counterfeit case and little did I think at the time it would turn out to be an adventure.

Someone in a mid-western city had an informant who wanted to introduce an agent to a suspect who had counterfeit money. The suspect, Adrian, came from a family who controlled most of the crime in that particular city. He had the reputation of being a killer. I took a younger agent with me at the time and met the informant in a diner on the outskirts of the city.

While we were there discussing the case, Adrian came into the diner. The informant made the necessary introductions and after being introduced to the younger agent, Adrian turned on his heels and walked out of the diner. I told the informant to chase after Adrian and find out what was wrong. The informant returned in a few minutes and said that Adrian did not like the younger agent; that he looked too much like a "cop" and it made him nervous. I told the agent to wait for me in the car outside and then chased after Adrian and talked with him in the parking lot. He reiterated that the other man made him nervous and he would not do business as long as he was around. I explained that this fellow was just released from jail and that he was making a few bucks driving me around. I assured him that he was okay and that he would not be around for a deal if it made him nervous. Adrian apologized for his actions but insisted that the other agent not be present when a deal was consummated. We then went back into the diner and made arrangements for a delivery of counterfeit money that evening in the diner. Adrian explained that he had ten thousand dollars in counterfeit money remaining. He did not like handling counterfeit notes and this was going to be his last sale. I complained that I could not get rich on a ten thousand dollar buy and was hoping to make purchases in the future. Adrian stated that after this deal was completed, he would call his connection and let me speak with him on the telephone. I could then make future purchases directly from his connection. He stated that he did not want to have anything further to do with counterfeit.

Some hours later a car drove up to the diner. Adrian left and got a package from the car, met me in the men's room, gave me the notes and was paid. He then went to the public phone booth in the diner and called his connection on the telephone. He put me on with a man called Butch. Butch told me that I could call him in a week or so. I left Adrian and thanked him for letting me talk with his connection.

About a week later, I called Butch on the telephone and made arrangements to go out to see him. I arrived in town and he told me to meet him at a private, after-hours club in town. I went to the club and a man called Tony told me that Butch would see me in a couple of hours. Tony was interested in where I came from and who I knew. He had a patch across his nose and I asked him if he was a "pug." He said no, that he just had his nose remodeled and expected to take the bandages off in a couple of days.

Butch finally came into the club and we had a conversation. For some reason, Butch and I did not get along too well. He wanted money in advance and wanted me to wait a few days for delivery. He, however, admitted he was the source of the notes that Adrian delivered to me. After several hours, I decided I could not do business with Butch and I told him I was leaving town and I would call him at a later date. I then went back to the office and a few days later had a consultation with the United States Attorney handling the district where the buy was made. He was delighted because Adrian was a target for all police officers in that particular area and no one was very successful in making a case against him. The United States Attorney stated that Butch could be brought in on a conspiracy and it would not be necessary to wait until another buy was made.

A short time later, I testified before the grand jury and the indictments were expected to be handed down in a matter of two or three weeks.

A couple of days later, I was working in a small New England town on straight investigations. That night I stopped in a State Police barracks to spend an evening with some old friends. The sergeant and I were playing rummy in his office. When he excused himself to answer a phone, I picked up the clip board that had all the wanted persons on it. The top flyer caught my eye, "Wanted for Murder" etc. After examining the picture I felt that this was the picture of Tony, perhaps before his "nose job." The flyer was put out by a small city in New England. The more I examined the picture, the more I was convinced that it was Tony. I took an awful ribbing from the troopers who accused me of getting old and trying to make one more case before retirement.

The next morning, I put a call into the department that was responsible for the flyer. The lieutenant in charge of the department was delighted. He stated that the flyer was out for over a year and this was the first lead he received on it. I made arrangements to meet him in New York City the following day.

The next day, I met the lieutenant and the sergeant in charge of homicide. They related how Tony was a suspect in a particular horrible rape-murder case. They showed me photos of the victim and there was no doubt that it was a vicious crime. I then related how I got involved in the case. When I mentioned the name of Adrian, the lieutenant snapped his fingers and said, "that does it."

Adrian is the nephew of Tony and there is no doubt the man you met in the private club is our man.

I then made arrangements with our headquarters to be allowed to work with the local police to run down Tony and to start at the private club. I had just made all the arrangements when I received a telephone call from the United States Attorney handling the counterfeit case that indictments were handed down and Adrian and Butch were arrested. This certainly canceled anything I could do in an undercover capacity, because now both Adrian and Butch knew I was an agent. We all felt that neither Butch nor Adrian would plead guilty as both had long records. As a matter of fact, Adrian was on probation for burglary in New York State for ten years and could not stand a conviction on the counterfeit case because he would then have to serve the ten years for violation.

The lieutenant and sergeant were down in the dumps when they left but I assured them I felt something would happen and we would come up with Tony. The arrest of Adrian and Butch would undoubtedly send Tony underground and straight investigation would not produce him. Somewhere along the line, we had to make a deal. I felt fairly sure if the cards were played right, Adrian would supply the answer.

Several months later, the case was called for trial in the mid-west. I took the stand and testified as to my conversation with Adrian and the subsequent purchase of counterfeit notes from him. I then told of my meeting with Butch in which he admitted being the source of the notes handled by Adrian. The younger agent who was with me at the original meeting testified about seeing Adrian get a package from a car that pulled up in front of the diner. After a few more witnesses, the government rested. The defense had no witnesses. The next day, the case went to the jury who promptly returned a verdict of guilty against both defendants. The judge delayed sentencing until the following day and the defendants were continued on bail.

That evening I received a call from Adrian's lawyer telling me that Adrian wanted to meet me somewhere alone. I felt that maybe this was what we were waiting for, a deal from Adrian. Then again, with Adrian's reputation for being a killer, this could be a setup and his way to get even with me. I decided to risk it and I contacted the lawyer and told him that I would meet Adrian alone in a small bar about ten miles out of town. Naturally, I made the necessary arrangements for cover for myself while meeting with Adrian.

Adrian kept the appointment and immediately informed me that he knew I did not come alone. He said it made no difference because he had a favor to ask me. I asked him what it was. Adrian said that his lawyer wanted to make it known to the judge that the notes handled by him were his last venture in counterfeiting and that he had nothing to do with my trip to meet Butch and was not to get any part of the profits. I told him my job was not to work for the defense but that I would discuss it with the United States Attorney the following morning and I felt sure that he would not oppose what his lawyer said.

He then told me how worried he was about his probation violation and he thought he could never do ten years and then a federal sentence on the counterfeiting charge. When he was about ready to leave, I told him I had a favor to ask him. He smiled and said, "what?" I said, "tell me where Uncle Tony is." He looked as though he was going to faint. He said, "what do you know about my uncle Tony and how could you as a Federal Officer be interested in him." I quieted Adrian down a bit and told him that Tony was only an uncle by marriage, for the last year he probably was not supporting his wife, and further, a man who would rape and mutilate a girl the way he did was certainly not worth protecting. Adrian said, "its not as easy as you think. If my father thought I had anything to do with turning in my uncle he would personally cut my throat. That's for sure."

The next day in court, Adrian was sentenced to serve six years in a Federal penitentiary. He had three hours to surrender and again he made it his business to meet me in the washroom in the courthouse. He shook hands with me and said, "if I ever decide to go along with you, will you promise that I will only deal with you and no one else will know of my cooperation?" I said I would handle it the best way I knew how. I cautioned him not to contact me unless it was to help with locating his uncle. We shook hands and we parted.

A probation warrant was promptly filed against him and for all purposes, the matter was laid to rest. In the meantime, Adrian gave the whole matter serious thought while he was serving time in the federal penitentiary. He thought of the six years to be followed by ten years in a state prison and it did not take long for Adrian to make up his mind.

One day, while spending my vacation at a lakeside cottage in upstate New York, I received a telephone call from my office stating that the warden of the Federal penitentiary wanted me to call him. I called the warden and he told me that a prisoner, Adrian, wanted to see me and I would know what it was all about.

I immediately got in touch with the lieutenant and sergeant who were carrying the case and told them that I was sure we would be coming up with Tony. We all drove out to the penitentiary and the officers waited outside while it was arranged that I speak to Adrian in private. The warden was a very understanding man and he made things as easy as possible for us. Adrian told me that he was finding the time very hard to serve and wanted to know if I could get the probation warrant canceled and arrange to have his federal time cut to time served. I told him he was driving too hard a bargain and I could not handle it. We finally agreed that I would try to have the probation warrant lifted and for that he would let me know where I could find his uncle. He stated that he would not make a move until I came back personally and gave my word that the warrant was lifted.

I left him and joined the sergeant and lieutenant who were waiting outside. I told them of the bargain I made. They said, "where do we go from here." I said, "lets go to see the judge that issued the warrant and see if he will help us."

Off we went about one thousand miles away. Inquiries by me in the town revealed that the judge was really tough, especially on probation violators who had been given an opportunity to go straight. We were having a sandwich in a restaurant, trying to figure out the next move. We had a problem here involving five different states and it was becoming harder to solve. While we were talking, in walked a state police lieutenant, the man who was a sergeant when I first looked at the wanted flyer. He was a "sight for sore eyes" and I brought him up to date on the development of the case. He said he knew the judge and would accompany us to his chambers and try to help.

We saw the judge and he certainly was tough. He said he understood our problem but he could not in good conscience "pull the warrant." Fortunately, the lieutenant was carrying the photographs of the corpse with him. I asked the lieutenant to show the pictures to the judge. He looked at them and they almost turned his stomach. I told the judge I wanted to trade the man who committed that murder for a cheap burglar. The judge understood and said he would "pull the warrant" providing we caught the murderer. In a short time, we headed back to the penitentiary in far better spirits than we left.

The following day, I arranged to see Adrian. I told him that I had a firm commitment that the warrant would be withdrawn if we could arrest the murderer. Adrian scowled at me and said, "who ever said I would help a cop. I'm no rat, get out of here." With that he threw an old match box cover at me and stormed out of the room. I did not know what to think, I picked up the match box cover and on the inside was written a name, address and social security number. I left the prison, went outside and told the lieutenant and sergeant that I thought I had the answer but was not sure. For some reason, Adrian could not bring himself to tell me where his uncle was. He put it on the back of the match box cover and threw it at me. On second thought, perhaps he thought the room was bugged or he was being watched and this was the only way he could protect himself.

The city written on the cover was about 950 miles away, so off we went again. We went to the address and knocked on the door. It was answered by none other than Adrian's uncle, the man wanted for murder. He immediately recognized the lieutenant. He said he was glad the hunt was over and voluntarily accompanied the lieutenant and sergeant back to stand trial for the murder. I took the plane back and continued on my vacation. I tried to explain to my wife why I was gone for more than the day I had promised her.

Q: Is it a good idea to write down everything an informant tells you?

A: I guess there are times when a law enforcement officer has to take out his pad and write down the entire interview he has

Figure 15. Seizure of counterfeit notes and weapons. Left to right: D. P. Hollman, Chief Joint Strike Force; A. E. Whitaker, Dept of Justice; author, and H. Gibbs, Special Agent in charge.

with a witness or possible suspect. However, when talking to an informant, it is a very bad policy to whip out the book and start writing. This is very official looking and most informants think that they will be held to everything they say. The best system is to have an informal conversation with the informant, possibly in a restaurant or other place, get to know each other and after the conversation is ended, the officer should then go back to the office and try to reconstruct the conversation or at least the pertinent parts. If there are addresses and telephone numbers that he needs, he can get them on a subsequent conversation with the informant. Regardless of what an informant tells an officer, the officer should not show any emotions and should act like the priest in a confessional, as if he has heard it all and nothing surprises him. I recall a conversation that a rather new agent had with an informant, it went something like this.

Informant: I know where there is a lot of counterfeit money.

Agent: Yeah? Like how much?

Informant: Maybe as much as a million dollars.

Agent: Wowie! You're not kidding are you? Boy, I never saw that much money in my whole life. Let's go and get it. I'll bet it will be the biggest case we ever made.

Informant: Wait a minute. This involves a lot of people.

Agent: Like who?

Informant: Petey White, Horsey Phillips and Joe Cataldo.

Agent: Who are they?

Informant: They are all Mafia connected.

Agent: Wowieeee! Let me at them. Boy, if you can get me those guys and that money, I'll be made. Gosh, I'd give anything to make a case like that.

Informant: Well, I can do it but it's gonna cost you etc., etc.

We can spend an entire chapter on the mistakes that the agent was making in handling this informant. In the first place, he was too emotional. When he heard a million dollars he got excited and showed his feelings to the informant. When he mentioned that this was perhaps the biggest case, he was practically telling the informant to ask for the largest reward they ever paid. He asked the informant for the names of the people involved, then admitted he never heard of them. Then he got all excited because the informant mentioned that they were all "connected people." As the conversation went on, the informant also got carried away with his own importance because of the actions of the agent and it was not long before the informant was trying to run the whole case. It became necessary to bring another agent in with the informant, explain to the informant that the other agent was new and it would take a more experienced man to handle this case. It took hours to correct the errors made by the first agent. The new man would have been in much better shape by just getting the facts and reporting them to his superior for analysis before he became all excited. It will be interesting to note, that this informant was a big "blowhard" and he made an insignificant case. He was paid for more than he deserved and never proved useful thereafter.

Q: How do you pick the proper man for a particular undercover case?

A: At best, this is a hit and miss proposition. When you are a supervisor you know the particular talents of the men working for you. Some men are best suited for working with a particular ethnic group. Some men are only good for the small cases. Others can only work the big ones, either because of looks, dress, attitude or ethnic background. With any group of men, it soon becomes evident after several cases, the ones they are best suited for. Again, there are times when you have to take a man because he never worked in a particular neighborhood and hence might not be known. Sometimes manpower shortages dictate using whatever agent is available. I find if I cannot make up my mind what agent to use, I will let the informant pick the man he would like to work with. Generally, his suggestion is excellent, as he knows who the suspects are and how well a certain person will fit in with the group. If for any reason the case does not work out, you will not have to listen to the informant tell you that you sent the wrong man on the case.

Q: If you trust an informant, should you tell him what you know about a certain case?

A: You have to be very careful about telling an informant

about a certain case. Whether you trust him or not, you should *not* give him information unless it is important that he has this information to successfully work the case. To give him any additional information serves no purpose other than to make him knowledgeable and put him in a position to bargain, perhaps with the other side. To "boil it all down," the answer is — an informant is supposed to give information to police, police are not supposed to give information to informants.

Q: What do you think of a hearing aid as a prop?

A: Normally a hearing aid should not make a person too suspicious, unless he is very knowledgeable and knows that a hearing aid could be converted into a transmitter and be used as a technical police device. Let us say a man uses a hearing aid as a prop, he is successful and that particular group learns that they have been victimized. Can you imagine how much success the next undercover agent will have if he decides to use a similar device? I put a hearing aid in the category as a "one shotter." If used on a case successfully, it should be a long time before it is used again.

Q: In a successful undercover case, who receives the credit for the case?

A: Statistics are a necessary evil and they must be used in police work just the same as in any business. Unfortunately, all police departments are fighting the battle of the budget and must show someone how successful they are to get enough money to operate. In this sense, statistics are very important. In an undercover case, many people go into the success of the case. The informant, the covering agents, the arresting agents, and finally the undercover agent. Regardless how you set up your credits, the undercover agent will always be singled out as the man who gets the lion's share of the credit. Undercover work captures the imagination of everyone, including the defendants, the judge, the district attorney and the jury. He takes the most chances and naturally, will receive the most credit. I personally would like to see a group get the credit. To make a successful case, the entire team must function smoothly and know exactly what to do under any set of circumstances and always be in a position to protect the undercover agent at any time during the case. To sum it up, while the undercover agent will receive most of the credit for a successful case, the case can only be made with the efforts of an entire smooth-working team. There should be enough credit for the whole team.

Q: Suppose you are working an undercover counterfeit case and the suspect shows you a genuine note as a sample, should you let him know that you are aware that the note is genuine?

A: No, not right away. Nothing would be gained by letting him know that you are an expert in detecting genuine or counterfeit money. This might make him suspicious that you know more than you should. He might then suspect that you are an agent. There is no harm in remarking that the note looks very good and you hope that the notes that are delivered are of the same excellent quality. He has a purpose in showing you a genuine note, it may be that he cannot get samples and has no intention of delivering notes to you. The notes that he intends to deliver may be of such poor quality he is afraid that you would not buy them if you saw one of the samples. Showing you genuine notes as samples might put him in a position of asking a much higher price because the merchandise is so good. I recall an occasion where it became necessary to let the man know that the samples were genuine. The case ran something like this.

The suspect had me meet him in an upstate motel room. He was a legitimate business man who was 90 per cent legitimate and 10 per cent thief. He was acting as a commission man between a band of known thieves and myself. At first he was interested in selling stolen stock certificates as he had a Wall Street background and was very knowledgeable about stock, bonds, etc.

Somewhere along the line, his people told him they could get counterfeit money in any amounts. The switch from stocks to counterfeit money was done without any warning and I immediately became suspicious. This particular subject and myself were not getting along too well. His prices were always too high. He never did anything of value and I began to suspect that while he was anxious to make a sale, perhaps the people behind him were trying to pull a stick up. However, I told him I was interested in the counterfeit notes and he stated that he would have some samples and prices for me the following day. He went into a long discussion of how his people had invested a fortune in this scheme and were anxious to make a large sale.

A day or two later, we met again in a hotel room and he showed me two brand new five dollar bills. He pointed out to me that the bills each bore the same serial number, and therefore were counterfeit. I examined the bills and immediately knew that they were genuine bills. They did bear identical serial numbers, however, I noted that they had removed the last number from each serial number on the bill. These bills were brand new and originally had consecutive numbers on them. One bill was B 80756701C and the other was B 80756702C. Erase the last number on each bill and both bills would read B 8075670 C. The extra space before the last letter would hardly be noticeable to anyone not familiar with money.

I was sure that this man really believed that the notes were counterfeit. I agreed that they looked very good and tried to arrive at a price. He wanted something like thirty-five cents on a dollar for "lots" of 100,000 dollars. He wanted the buy money in advance and wanted to effect a sale immediately. We were arguing about the price when I received a telephone call from the covering agents. They advised me that there was a Cadillac full of "hoods" waiting near the entrance of the hotel and that they were undoubtedly trying to pull a stick up, if they were convinced that I had any large amount of money. Armed with this information, I went back to negotiating with the suspect in the room. He kept on saying that these people had invested a fortune in making these notes and that it was done just for me and that I was obligated to do business their way and as quickly as possible. I pretended that I was examining the samples and luckily I had two consecutively numbered notes in my own money. While he was talking, I made it appear that suddenly it struck me that there was a swindle brewing. I turned to him and said, "how much did your people invest in this set up?" He said a "small" fortune. I then opened the desk, took out a pencil with an eraser and proceeded to erase the last number of the bills I had in my possession. When I finished, I threw the bills in his face and said very theatrically, "your people invested exactly three cents for an eraser and one minute of their time." I then grabbed him by the throat and tried to get him to admit that he was part of the swindle. He assured me he was not and began to worry that his people were up to something.

He said he would have a hard time convincing the people that I did not want the counterfeit money. He felt reasonably sure that this was, in fact, a stickup and being a businessman he did not want to become involved. He finally left my room a shaken man and went back to his people with a story that he did not trust me and that no deal could be arranged.

The mob "hit him up for a good piece of change," supposedly for the trouble they went through. We kept good relations with the suspect and finally another agency set him up for a large amount of stolen stock certificates. He and his associates were arrested during the delivery of over a million dollars worth of stolen stocks.

Information later leaked out that the counterfeit scheme was just that and they had no idea of delivering counterfeit money. They thought that they could pull a stick up in the hotel room on a man who was engaged in an illegal venture and probably would not even report it to the police.

Q: Would it be proper to let one informant know that another person is an informant and supplying information on the same case?

A: Absolutely not. An informant should be used for the purpose of obtaining information and should never be in a position where he is getting information from the agency he is working with. If you told him that another person is giving you information, he will feel that at a future date, you might reveal his cooperation to another person. Most informants will respect the fact that you will not give them any information and that you are noncommittal about anyone else giving you information.

Q: Does there ever come a time when it becomes necessary to drop an informant?

A: I am sure that everyone has had the experience where they feel an informant is not worth working with or that sometime in the past he has double-crossed them and they reach a point where they will not work with him under any circumstances. I hate to think that this happens too often. In my experience I can think of only two or three cases where I would not use a particular informant, not because of what he had done in the past but because I knew the information he was giving me was not true and he was merely playing for time, generally because of an impending prison term which he was trying to forestall. There is no magic way of telling whether an informant is leveling with you. You have to hear him out, evaluate what he tells you and match that with what you already know and then come to a decision as to whether or not you can trust the man. Past performances will play an important part in making up your mind but this should never be the determining factor.

Juan was known to our office for about five years. He was an addict and came around to the office when he was really desperate for money. He invariably came to the office with stories about counterfeit note distributing in his neighborhood. However, he was never able to bring in a counterfeit note, or any kind of sample to show what was being sold in his area. Each time he came to the office he would manage to get a few dollars for expenses and generally nothing ever came of the information that he gave us. It soon became apparent to the agents working with him that he was becoming a "con man" and would invent stories just to get a little scratch.

One day he called the office and asked to have an agent meet him as he had some valuable information. At this time, Juan was not held in very high esteem and I doubt if any agent would have taken the time out to meet him several miles away. However, the telephone was answered by a comparatively new and very smart agent who took the time out to identify the informant. Because no one else was around, he went out of his way to meet him. Juan not only had counterfeiting information, five samples and a list of the people involved, but was also in a position to introduce a Spanish speaking agent to the group as a potential buyer. Juan was "throwing caution to the winds" because he had decided to leave the country and try to make a new life in the country of his birth. A good counterfeiting conspiracy was made and a very dangerous note was put out of circulation very early because we were fortunate in having an agent handle a matter who did not rely on past performance when handling an informant.

Q: Are there any advantages to having a delivery made in another location or another city away from where the suspect normally operates?

A: Changing cities provides an ideal situation for the undercover agent. Taking a suspect away from his home base puts him in a vulnerable situation. In his home town he probably knows most of the local police by sight. In the event he sees something he does not like, he will have no trouble getting someone to check it out. In the event of an arrest, he can contact friends and relatives to get a bondsman to put up bail. He can also get legal aid from his associates or friends. All these advantages are turned to disadvantages when he is arrested in a strange city. It is surprising how often a man is refused help by his associates when he is arrested out of town. Very often, they even resent the telephone call from the suspect as they fear the police are listening and may tie them into the particular crime. When violators languish in jail, especially in a strange city where there are no visitors and no word reaching them, they soon give some thought to cooperating with the authorities. They feel they have been "thrown to the wolves" and there is nothing to gain by keeping quiet. They begin to believe perhaps some of their own friends gave them up and begin to rationalize the reason for cooperating.

Several years ago, I was assigned to a city in the south-west to work with an informant on a counterfeit case. This particular informant was very high in the hierarchy of the underworld in the particular area and an introduction from him was all that was needed to make a successful case. This particular informant had a beautiful home, plenty of money, servants and everything that goes with a successful man.

He gave a Christmas party at his home and invited a lot of people to a gathering there just before the holidays. I appeared at the party when it was in full swing and during the course of the evening, the informant gave me a casual introduction to the suspect. We managed to get friendly and before the evening was over, the suspect let it be known to me that he could get counterfeit money in large amounts. I told him I was going back East and would like to take a couple of thousand dollars with me. He said he could arrange it as he had several thousand in his car. He went out and I met him in the basement of the home where the party was being held. We negotiated a sale with no trouble at all. He then gave me his home phone number and told me to call him at any time.

After the party was over, I talked with the informant and let him know that a buy had been consummated. The informant made sure never to mention my name in the future, and was laying the groundwork to let it be known that I was brought to the party by someone else.

About ten days later, I called the suspect and told him that my people were interested in 150,000 dollars worth of notes and asked him if he could get them. He said it would be no trouble and I could go out there anytime. I told him that my people wanted delivery in New York City and that they would pay the expenses to effect a delivery there. He said that he did not think he could arrange the delivery in New York City. I gave him a number where he could reach me and he said he would call me back.

We had contact by phone for several days thereafter and suddenly one day he called me and said that he thought he could make the delivery in New York City. He stated that his girl friend and another couple wanted to come to New York for a sort of vacation and he thought he could bring the notes with him and mix business with pleasure. I told him it would be fine and promised to get him tickets for shows, prize fights, night clubs, etc.

About two days later, the suspect arrived in town, registered at a local hotel and then called me. I, along with my "chauffeur" met them at the hotel. All four (two men and their girl friends) were conversant about the counterfeit money they had brought and were anxious to swing a deal so they could go out and enjoy themselves.

One of our Chinese agents had arranged through some Chinese friends to borrow the upstairs room in their restaurant in China Town. It was very easy for me to tell the suspects that we were going out for a Chinese dinner and that the owner of the restaurant was the man putting up the money for the counterfeits. The party was delighted and they accepted a lift from my chauffer to take them down to China Town. In the meantime, all was in readiness for them. The outer perimeter covered the street outside the restaurant and also the downstairs portion of the premises. The owner of the restaurant, and several agents posing as a part of the syndicate were upstairs preparing for the banquet. Before coming downtown to meet me, they went to a public garage and retrieved the counterfeit money from the trunk of their car. They then accompanied my man on the trip downtown. They arrived on schedule and came to the restaurant and were guided upstairs where the buyers were waiting for them. Needless to say, an arrest was effected at our leisure as the suspects were pretty well boxed in.

They were put in a Federal detention home for the night and the next day spent several futile hours trying to get in touch with friends and make bail. For some reason, there was no help forthcoming and twenty-four hours after they were arrested, they wanted to make a deal. They made it very clear that the only reason they were cooperating was because they were in a strange town with no friends and apparently their friends from out of town had abandoned them. Their cooperation was accepted and a deal was worked out. Again, several additional cases were made and eventually the plant was seized and the manufacturers were apprehended.

The point here was that the cooperation was offered solely because they felt they were abandoned. If the arrest had been made in their home town, there would have been no trouble arranging for a bondsman, lawyer, etc. It is interesting to note that other than the man who checked them into the hotel, every other person they met was a law enforcement official. When the arrest was made and they saw the picture, they realized how hopeless the situation was and then fully cooperated.

The informant in this case also came out "clean as a lily." When questioned, he said that he only met me for the first time at his home; that I was brought there by a mutual friend. The informant told the suspects that he resented being questioned because apparently, they had what they thought was a lucrative deal going and he was not told about it or was he going to get his cut. This was a case where just about everything turned out good for the "good guys."

Chapter 7

CONCLUSION

THE search for a better and more efficient way to fight crime is never-ending. There is more sophisticated equipment available to investigative agencies. Computers are giving us valuable information in a fraction of the time it used to take. Colleges and universities have taken up the challenge and are now giving degrees in police science. Foundations are offering large grants for research into crime and ways to combat it. Police organizations have pooled their assets to make a stronger assault against the criminal. Special units are being formed by City, State and Federal Governments to form a concentrated effort to fight organized crime. These are the positive sides of the ledger, on the opposite side we have recent court decisions which have complicated the policeman's everyday work. He is expected to make a decision in a split second and have this decision stand up in the various appeals courts and even in the Supreme Court. We have apathy on the part of the public who are not interested in suppressing crime until it hits close to home. We have low salaries in many police departments which prevent the department from getting more qualified personnel. Many officers today have to moonlight in order to make ends meet. There are officers who are appointed and who start their job with little or no training. There is also, in some cases, apathy on the part of the police officer himself, both the old timer and the newest recruit who are satisfied to hold down a job for the sake of the paycheck and could care less about detection and prevention of crime. The pendulum swings only so far in one direction and must change its position and inexorably head in the opposite direction. With all the new innovations in criminal investigations nothing has really changed in the basic concept of the work. Like the foot soldier in all the past wars, the police officer is the final bulwark in the fight against crime. Someone once said that "there is nothing new under the sun."

Perhaps the same can be said about police work. In order to solve a case, a suspect must be arrested and convicted. In order to convict a person there must be witnesses to testify. It is the policeman whose job it is to find the witness and produce him in court. In some cases it is the policeman himself who either has witnessed the crime or becomes a witness because he has worked undercover and can give testimony first-hand. This is the supreme effort any officer can make in the fight against crime, short of giving his life which on some occasions he is forced to do.

Much has been discussed about undercover work in this book. There is no doubt it is one of the more successful ways to fight crime. We have discussed that it is not an exact science and that it cannot be learned by reading books or sitting in classrooms. Over the years, certain techniques have been tried and discarded, others have been tried and retained. As the underworld became familiar with certain techniques they were reevaluated and other methods were found to stay one step ahead of the criminal. Undercover work has been used by the police officer with some degree of success over the years. Today, however, its very existence is threatened. Entrapment, the perennial plea in all undercover cases, is becoming more liberalized in its interpretation. At one time it would suffice to say "Did the suspect have the idea in his mind to commit the crime, or was the idea supplied by the undercover agent?" If the idea was in the mind of the suspect, then the entrapment plea did not apply. Basically, the law is the same today, however, recently a more liberalized interpretation has been seen in the courts, I can recall a conversation that I had with a judge some years ago in which he gave me his personal views on entrapment. The case he cited was as follows: Assume a man offered contraband to an undercover agent at a price of say three hundred dollars for the item. The agent refused to make the purchase because the price was too high. He makes a counter-offer of two hundred dollars which is accepted by the suspect. The judge felt that this could be considered entrapment because the original offer was not accepted. He felt that the refusal closed the first phase of the case. When the agent made an offer of two hundred dollars this was something new and because the offer was made by an agent of the Government, this constituted entrapment. The judge also felt that any time an undercover agent gave the suspect money in advance to obtain the contraband, this could also be considered entrapment because the suspect probably could have never purchased the contraband unless he used the money which was supplied by the undercover agent.

The judge went on to state that he realized he was in the minority on his views of entrapment and that it might be years before they were adopted. The good judge has since passed away and I hope his thoughts on "entrapment" are also laid to rest. If they are not, then undercover work which has played a major role in law enforcement will become a thing of the past and will hamper all agencies in their fight against crime.

INDEX